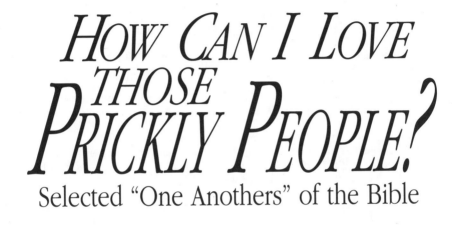

HOW CAN I LOVE THOSE PRICKLY PEOPLE?

Selected "One Anothers" of the Bible

JUANITA PURCELL

REGULAR BAPTIST PRESS
1300 North Meacham Road
Schaumburg, Illinois 60173-4806

Quotations on pages 8/9, 44, 45, 78, and 81 are from *My Utmost for His Highest* by Oswald Chambers. © 1935; Dodd, Mead & Co., renewed 1963 by the Oswald Chambers Publications Assn., Ltd. Used by permission of Discovery House Publishers, Box 3566, Grand Rapids, MI 49501. All rights reserved.

Quotations on pages 16 and 87/88 are from *The Bible Exposition Commentary,* vol. 1, by Warren W. Wiersbe. © 1989; SP Publications, Inc., Wheaton, IL 60187. Published by Victor Books. Used by permission.

Quotation on page 16 is from *The Word in Life Study Bible.* © 1993; Thomas Nelson, Inc. Used by permission.

Quotations on pages 24 and 26 are from *The Fruit of the Spirit* by Leroy Brownlow. © 1982, 1989 by Leroy Brownlow. Brownlow Publishing Company, Fort Worth, TX. Used by permission.

Quotation on page 29 is from *From the Father's Heart* by Charles Slagle. © 1989; Charles Slagle. Used by permission of Destiny Image Publishers, P. O. Box 351, Shippensburg, PA 17257.

Quotation on page 30 is from *God Is Enough,* edited by Melvin E. Dieter and Hallie A. Dieter. © 1986; Melvin E. Dieter and Hallie A. Dieter. Used by permission of Zondervan Publishing House.

Quotations on pages 36 and 37 are from *Rebuilding Your Broken World* by Gordon MacDonald. © 1988; Gordon MacDonald. Thomas Nelson Publishers. Used by permission.

Quotations on page 43 are from *Thoughts of Gold.* © 1974, 1990 by Leroy Brownlow. Brownlow Publishing Company, Fort Worth, TX. Used by permission.

Quotations on pages 50, 51, and 53 are from *The God of All Comfort* by Hannah Whitall Smith. 1956 edition. Moody Bible Institute of Chicago. Moody Press. Used by permission.

Quotation on page 60 is from *Sidetracked Home Executives* by Pam Young and Peggy Jones. © 1981; Pam Young and Peggy Jones. Reprinted by permission of Warner Books/New York.

Quotations on pages 68, 69/70, 71, and 81 are from "Selected Illustrations from *Bible Illustrator.*" © 1990–91; Parsons Technology, Inc. All rights reserved. Used by permission.

Quotations on pages 68/69 and 92 are from *Portraits of Perseverance* by Henry Gariepy. © 1989; SP Publications, Inc., Wheaton, IL 60187. Published by Victor Books. Used by permission.

Quotation on page 86 is from *Life Application Bible.* © 1988, 1989, 1990, 1991 by Tyndale House Publishers, Inc., Wheaton, IL 60189. Used by permission. All rights reserved. *Life Application* is a registered trademark of Tyndale House Publishers, Inc. New Testament Life Application Notes and Bible Helps © owned by assignment to Tyndale House Publishers, Inc. Used by permission. All rights reserved. Harmony of the Gospels © 1986 by James C. Galvin. Maps in text © 1986, 1988 by Tyndale House Publishers, Inc. All rights reserved. Used by permission of Tyndale House Publishers, Inc.

Quotations on pages 93, 95/96, and 97/98 are from *The Power of Encouragement* by Jeanne Doering. © 1982; Jeanne Doering. Moody Press. Used by permission.

HOW CAN I LOVE THOSE PRICKLY PEOPLE?
© 1995
Regular Baptist Press • Schaumburg, Illinois
1-800-727-4440
Printed in U.S.A.
All rights reserved

Fourth printing—2000

CONTENTS

A SPECIAL THANKS

To my mother, Imogene Reed, who assisted me with the last-minute paperwork and helped me get this book to the publisher on time.

PREFACE

Why do we need "one another" when Christ said He would never leave us or forsake us (Hebrews 13:5)? The Lord Jesus needs to be preeminent in the lives of believers (Colossians 1:18), but the Bible clearly teaches we need other believers to encourage us, to love us, to build us up. I once read of nine physically disabled people who climbed Mount Rainier. Despite the fact that five people were blind, two were deaf, one was epileptic, and one had an artificial leg, they all climbed to the top of the 14,000-foot mountain and made it back down. When asked how they accomplished this amazing feat, one of the blind members said, "We had a lot of help from one another." To some degree, each of us has a weakness in some area. We all need one another.

Who will help bear the burden of a fallen sister? Who will encourage her sister when all hope seems to be gone? Who will go the second mile to save a relationship? Will you? God has commanded us to do this! He wants us to be "one another" Christians.

We all know we should do it; the question is, How can we do it? What about the prickly, pestering, pouting people among us who aren't easy to love and care for? Can we relate to them? The Bible contains positive commands about what believers should be doing for others and what they should not be doing against others.

In a quick search of the New Testament, I found forty-three "one another" passages that could transform our lives. (If you check more thoroughly, you may find even more.) I have listed the verses under two headings on the following page.

Following Christ's example as given in these one another verses will make a definite difference in how we treat one another. In this study we will look at twelve of these commands in more detail.

DO

Love—John 13:34; Romans 13:8; 1 Thessalonians 3:12; 4:9; 1 John 3:11, 23; 4:7, 11, 12

Be kindly affectioned—Romans 12:10

Be kind—Ephesians 4:32

Be of the same mind—Romans 12:16

Be like-minded—Romans 15:5

Edify—Romans 14:19; 1 Thessalonians 5:11

Receive—Romans 15:7

Admonish—Romans 15:14; Colossians 3:16

Care for—1 Corinthians 12:25

Greet—1 Corinthians 16:20; 2 Corinthians 13:12; 1 Peter 5:14

Salute—Romans 16:16

Serve—Galatians 5:13

Forbear—Ephesians 4:2; Colossians 3:13

Forgive—Ephesians 4:32; Colossians 3:13

Submit—Ephesians 5:21; 1 Peter 5:5

Comfort—1 Thessalonians 4:18; 5:11

Show compassion—1 Peter 3:8

Minister to—1 Peter 4:10

Show hospitality—1 Peter 4:9

Exhort—Hebrews 3:13; 10:25

Consider—Hebrews 10:24

Confess faults—James 5:16

Pray for—James 5:16

Prefer—Romans 12:10

Bear burdens—Galatians 6:2

Wash feet—John 13:14

DON'T

Judge—Romans 14:13

Grudge—James 5:9

Consume—Galatians 5:15

Provoke—Galatians 5:26

Envy—Galatians 5:26

Lie—Colossians 3:9

Show partiality—1 Timothy 5:21

Speak evil—James 4:11

Love One Another

"A new commandment I give unto you, That ye love one another; as I have loved you, that ye also love one another"
(John 13:34).

Loving God is usually easy; loving people is work! It requires conscious and unconscious commitment twenty-four hours a day. Even the most lovable people are hard to love at one time or another. So why bother to love others when they probably will end up hurting you at some point in your life? Why bother? Because God commands it!

I enjoy the Godspeed program on my computer. I typed in "love one another," and, with one keystroke, I discovered that "love one another" appears nineteen times in the New Testament. Isn't that neat! Wouldn't it be great if we could carry out the command as easily as I could get that information?

Keeping the command to "love one another" is vitally important in our relationship to God and to others. John 14:15 says, "If ye love me, keep my commandments." Many people say, "I love God," but do they really? If you were to ask for evidence of their love for God, you might get these answers: "I go to church every Sunday"; "I read my Bible every day"; "I give my tithe every week." I know people who do all these things—but they won't speak to their next-door neighbors because they say they can't stand them. I know a person who won't allow her sister-in-law in her home because she doesn't like the way the sister-in-law acts. I heard of a professing Christian who hasn't spoken to her father in thirty years because he disapproved of her marriage. Do these ladies really know what God's kind of love is all about? Do you? Let's find out how God says we are to "love one another."

Why must we love one another?
1. Can a person have a right relationship with God and hate

7

her next-door neighbor or her father? Read 1 John 4:20 and 21. Explain your answer.

"One's love for God is equal to the love one has for the man he loves least." [1]

---

2. What was the setting when Christ gave the command to love one another in John 13:34? Read John 13:1–5, 31–35.

3. To love others was not a new command to the disciples; they had heard this before. Use a Bible concordance to find the first Biblical reference to loving your neighbor as yourself.

4. What does "love thy neighbour as thyself" mean?

5. Loving one another was not a new command, but Christ added to it. What was new about His command in John 13:34?

"The first thing God does is to knock pretence and the pious pose right out of me. The Holy Spirit reveals that God loved me not because I was lovable, but because it was His nature to do so. Now, He says to me, show the same love to others —'Love as I have loved you.' 'I will bring any

number of people about you whom you cannot respect, and you must exhibit My love to them as I have exhibited it to you.' You won't reach it on tiptoe. *Some of us have tried to, but we were soon tired.*

. . . Neither natural love nor Divine love will remain unless it is cultivated. Love is spontaneous, but it has to be maintained by discipline." [2]

6. Was this command just for the disciples? Who is a disciple of Christ?

7. When we show the kind of love commanded in John 13:34 and 35, what will people know about us?

"The Apostle John makes love for our fellow Christians to be a test of true faith, insisting that as we grow in grace we grow in love toward all of God's people: 'Every one that loveth him that begat loveth him also that is begotten of him' (1 John 5:1). This means simply that if we love God we will love His children. All true Christian experience will deepen our love for other Christians!

Therefore we conclude that whatever tends to separate us in person or in heart from our fellow Christians is not of God, but is of the flesh or of the devil." [3]

How must we love one another?

Christ said we are to love others the way He loves us. The Greek word for the kind of love Christ has for others is *agape. Agape* means "seeking the greatest good of another person."

8. In seeking the greatest good for us, what did Christ do? Read Ephesians 5:25.

Agape love is described in 1 Corinthians 13:4–8. This is the kind of love we are to have for one another.

9. Read 1 Corinthians 13:4–8. Summarize each of the characteristics of love from that passage with one word.

• Love suffers long (v. 4). _____

• Love is kind (v. 4). _____

• Love doesn't envy (v. 4). _____

• Love doesn't vaunt itself (v. 4). _____

• Love isn't puffed up (v. 4). _____

• Love doesn't behave itself in an unseemly way (v. 5).

_____

• Love doesn't seek its own (v. 5). _____

• Love isn't easily provoked (v. 5). _____

• Love thinks no evil (v. 5). _____

• Love doesn't rejoice in iniquity (v. 6). _____

• Love rejoices in the truth (v. 6). _____

• Love bears all things (v. 7). _____

• Love believes all things (v. 7). _____

• Love hopes all things (v. 7). _____

• Love endures all things (v. 7). _____

• Love never fails (v. 8). _____

10. How many of these characteristics describe your life? What are your strengths? What are your weaknesses?

PERFECT LOVE

Slow to suspect—quick to trust
Slow to condemn—quick to justify
Slow to offend—quick to defend
Slow to expose—quick to shield
Slow to reprimand—quick to forbear
Slow to belittle—quick to appreciate
Slow to demand—quick to give
Slow to provoke—quick to conciliate
Slow to hinder—quick to help
Slow to resent—quick to forgive [4]

After studying 1 Corinthians 13, you may be prone to respond something like this: "I can never live like that; it is too idealistic! I've tried a thousand times to live up to those standards. I just can't!"

11. What must happen in our lives before we have the power to practice this kind of love? Read 1 Peter 1:22 and 23.

12. Has your love for others changed since you've been born again? Recall an experience where God enabled you to love the unlovely.

13. If you are still saying, "I just can't love that person," maybe you are trying to do it in your own strength. How can we do things beyond our strength? Read Philippians 4:19 and Isaiah 40:31.

> *"It is natural to love them that love us, but it is supernatural to love them that hate us."* [5]

14. Now that you have studied this lesson, write your understanding of what it means to love one another as Christ loves us.

♡ *From My Heart*

What does love look like? Love looks like Jesus! How often do I look like Jesus in the way I treat others? Some days my grade would be good, but other days my score would be zero. Still, I am finding that my love for others has increased as my love for Christ has increased. So if you are having a hard time loving others, get to know Christ better. The more you know Him, the more you love Him; the more you love Him, the more you can love others.

It might be well if we sang this old hymn each day as a daily prayer:

> More love to Thee, O Christ, More love to Thee!
> Hear Thou the prayer I make On bended knee;
> This is my earnest plea:
> More love, O Christ, to Thee,
> More love to Thee, More love to Thee!

Elizabeth Prentiss not only wrote the words to this song, she lived out the words in her life. If you want to be challenged and blessed, read *Stepping Heavenward,* the story of her life. She lets us read portions of her daily diary and reveals her struggles in getting to know her Savior in a personal way.

Remember, the more you love Christ, the more you will be able to love others. Try it; it works!

From Your Heart

Whom are you having a hard time loving? Why must you love that person? What have you learned from this lesson that will help you love that person? Try praying for that person each day. As you pray for the person, and as you ask God to give you strength to obey His command, you will find yourself loving someone whom you thought you could not love.

Notes:
1. John J. Hugo, quoted by Eleanor Doan, compiler, *The Speaker's Sourcebook* (Grand Rapids: Zondervan Publishing House, 1960), p. 155.

2. Oswald Chambers, *My Utmost for His Highest* (New York: Dodd, Mead & Co., 1935), p. 132.

3. A. W. Tozer, quoted by G. B. Smith, compiler, *Renewed Day by Day* (Grand Rapids: Baker Book House, 1980), December 22.

4. Benjamin R. De Jong, *Uncle Ben's Quotebook* (Irvine, CA: Harvest House Publishers, 1976), p. 226.

5. De Jong, p. 224.

LESSON 2
Don't Judge One Another

"Let us not therefore judge one another any more: but judge this rather, that no man put a stumblingblock or an occasion to fall in his brother's way" (Romans 14:13).

You can feel the tension in the air at the church business meeting. The pastor brings before the saddened church the problem of a member who is involved in an immoral lifestyle. A deacon states he feels the church should make the girl and the other young people realize that the church does not approve of this kind of immoral conduct. Another angry member stands up and says, "I thought the Bible said we are not to judge one another. I thought we were to be loving and forgiving. God is the judge, not us!"

People who use Matthew 7:1, "Judge not, that ye be not judged," to say we are to love everyone and judge no one have taken the verse out of context. It is one thing to say, "Sally has done a bad thing"; it is quite different to say, "Sally is a bad person." Let's find out what God means when He says we are not to judge one another.

Is all judging wrong?
1. Matthew 7:1 must be understood in light of the context.
    (a) What is the "context" of a verse?

    (b) What does it mean to take a verse out of context?

2. (a) What is the context of Matthew 7:1? What is the setting? See Matthew 5:1.

14

(b) What do we often call Matthew 5, 6, and 7? (Check the subject headings in your Bible.)

3. What does it mean to "judge" another person?

4. In your experience, how widespread is the problem of judging others?

5. According to Matthew 7:2, how are we judged?

6. Read Matthew 7:3–5. Why did Jesus call His listeners "hypocrites"?

"As one writer put it, 'Most of us are umpires at heart; we like to call balls and strikes on somebody else.' The trouble is, it's pretty hard to call a game with a plank in our eye (Matt. 7:3-5).

For some of us, judging is a sporadic problem, a harsh word spoken without thought, an unfounded opinion that is quickly forgotten. But for others, it's a lifelong habit. We keep looking for signs of weakness in the people around us, constantly evaluating their attractiveness, their intel-

ligence, their charisma, and—what's worse—their spirituality." [1]

7. What does Matthew 7:3–5 teach us about judging?

> *"After we have judged ourselves honestly before God, and have removed those things that blind us, then we can help others and properly judge their works. But if we know there are sins in our lives, and we try to help others, we are hypocrites." [2]*

8. What would be a good guideline to follow in judging others? Read Matthew 7:12.

> *"When we are called upon to correct others, we should act like a good doctor whose purpose is to bring healing—not like an enemy who attacks." [3]*

9. What was to be judged according to Matthew 7:15–23?

10. What did Paul command the church in Corinth to do? Read 1 Corinthians 5:1–7.

Is your judgment based on principle or preference?

We sometimes major on the minors. Relationships are broken and churches are divided over issues that are insignificant in comparison to the vital issues of our lives and Christian faith.

11. Read Romans 14:13–23. What was happening in the church at Rome?

12. On what basis do some Christians today judge other Christians as less spiritual than themselves?

> Has God deserted Heaven,
> And left it up to you,
> To judge if this or that is right,
> And what each one should do?
>
> I think He's still in business,
> And knows when to wield the rod,
> So when you're judging others,
> Just remember, you're not—God. [4]

13. What can this kind of judging do to a church? Read Romans 14:20.

14. What is the difference between judging based on principle and judging based on preference?

15. Give an example of judging based on a clear Biblical principle and judging based on personal preference.

What is the right attitude in judging?

16. Read Matthew 7:1–5 again and Romans 14:13. What attitude does the Bible condemn when it says, "Judge not"?

17. Paul wrote to the Corinthians about the importance of each Christian's judging himself. Read 1 Corinthians 11:28–32. (a) What is one time when this judging should take place?

    (b) The early Christians observed the Lord's Supper daily; many of our churches observe it monthly. Is once-a-month personal judging sufficient?

18. What do we need to do about the sin we find when we judge, or examine, ourselves? Read 1 John 1:9.

> Tell not abroad another's faults
> Till thou hast cured thine own;
> Nor whisper of thy neighbor's sin
> Till thou art perfect grown:
> Then, when thy soul is pure enough
> To bear My searching eye
> Unshrinking, then may come the time
> Thy brother to decry. . . . [5]

♡ *From My Heart*

Do you ever judge others as less spiritual than you because they do things you don't do or go places you wouldn't go? They use taped background music in their church, and you don't; they use a different Bible translation than you do; they have drama in their church, and you don't.

I'm not condemning or condoning any of the above issues, but I believe they are preferences—not Biblical principles. Unfortunately, sometimes we make the non-essentials the essentials when God doesn't. How can believers who strongly disagree on nonessentials relate to one another without a judgmental, condemning attitude? We must remember that all born-again believers are part of the Body of Christ and servants of the same Lord and Master. We do not have the right to judge each other's spirituality; only the Lord has that right! He alone has the wisdom and knowledge to accurately evaluate the practices and opinions of other believers who differ from us.

We will all give an account to Him one day. "But why dost thou judge thy brother? or why dost thou set at nought thy brother? for we shall all stand before the judgment seat of Christ" (Romans 14:10). The Lord Who knows our motives, thoughts, and beliefs will impartially judge each of us. In the meantime, we need to spend more time judging ourselves and less time judging one another!

From Your Heart

Do you have a judgmental attitude toward someone? If it regards spiritual matters, is your judgment based on a Biblical principle or your preference? What have you learned about judging one another from this study?

Notes:

1. "Judge Not," *Moody* (January 1994), p. 13.

2. Warren W. Wiersbe, *The Bible Exposition Commentary,* vol. 1 (Wheaton, IL: Victor Books, 1989), p. 30.

3. *The Word in Life Study Bible* (Nashville: Thomas Nelson Publishers, 1993), p. 32.

4. Charles L. Allen, *God's Psychiatry* (Old Tappan, NJ: Fleming H. Revell Co., 1953), p. 116.

5. Lyra Mystica, quoted by Mary Wilder Tileston, compiler, *Joy and Strength* (Minneapolis: World Wide Publications, 1986), p. 13.

Be Kind to One Another

*"And be ye kind one to another, tenderhearted, forgiving one
another, even as God for Christ's sake hath forgiven you"
(Ephesians 4:32).*

Nothing is appreciated more in our relationships with
one another than the simple art of being kind. For some
people, kindness seems to come naturally; for most of us, it
is something we need to develop. Christians should be kind
because kindness is a fruit of the Spirit that God wants to
develop in our lives. "But the fruit of the Spirit is love, joy,
peace, longsuffering, gentleness, goodness, faith, meekness,
temperance: against such there is no law" (Galatians 5:22
and 23). The word "gentleness" in verse 22 is also translated
"kindness."

This wicked world is difficult enough without the
turmoil caused by sour, unkind people. A little kindness
goes a long way in smoothing touchy situations and prickly
people. Our kindness can add a touch of joy in an unhappy
world.

Kindness Defined

1. Look up the definition of kindness in the dictionary.
   After reading the definition, write your description of a
   kind person.

2. Who is the first person who comes to your mind when
   you think of kindness? Why?

"Kindness is love doing little things, things that seem scarcely worth doing, and yet which mean much to those for whom they are wrought. Kindness lends a hand when another is burdened. It speaks the cheerful word when a heart is discouraged. It gives a cup of cold water when one is thirsty. It is always doing good turns to somebody. It goes about performing little ministries with a touch of blessing. It scatters its favors everywhere. Few qualities do more to make a life bright and beautiful! Lord, make me kind today, full of love!

Scatter then your seeds of kindness, all enriching as you go—
Leave them. Trust the Harvest Giver; He will make each seed to grow.
So until the happy end, your life shall never lack a friend." [1]

3. The key verse for this lesson is Ephesians 4:32. What other characteristics follow kindness?

4. We will deal with the meaning of forgiveness in lesson 11, but what does it mean to be tenderhearted?

5. Someone has said, "In order to continually demonstrate a spirit of kindness, we must move off the judgment seat and onto the mercy seat." Why must we keep being kind toward others whom we feel don't deserve our kindness? Read Ephesians 4:32 again.

"In my daily life I am to ask, 'How would Christ have acted in my circumstances? How would He have me act? How would Christ fulfil [sic] my duties, do my work, fill my place, meet my difficulties, turn to account all my capacities and opportunities?' This is to be the law and inspiration of my whole life; not only of my outward acts, but of all my inward thoughts and desires. There is to be a manifestation of the Divine Nature in me." [2]

6. Henry Ward Beecher said, "Though the world needs reproof and correction, it needs kindness more; though it needs the grasp of the strong hand, it needs, too, the open palm of love and tenderness." What does that statement mean?

7. Most of us don't plan to be unkind; we just don't plan to be kind. How can we plan to be kind? Read Colossians 3:12.

". . . Before retiring to rest, and collecting our mind for our evening prayer, it were well to put these questions to our conscience, . . . 'Have I, in a single instance, shown sympathy or considerateness for others, borne with their faults or infirmities of character, given time or taken trouble to help them, or be of use to them?' If so, I have gained ground; I have made an advance in the mind of Christ to-day, if it be only a single step." [3]

8. Read 2 Peter 1:5–7. These verses tell us we must put on, or add, kindness to our lives. We develop one quality as

we exercise another quality. Why do you think kindness is listed before love?

9. Read Luke 6:31. How does this verse relate to showing kindness to one another?

10. Read Matthew 5:43–48. How are a believer and an unbeliever alike according to verses 46 and 47?

Kindness Demonstrated

11. In what kind of situations do you think kindness grows best?

> *"That misunderstanding, that mortification, that unkindness, that disappointment, that loss, that defeat,—all these are chariots waiting to carry you to the very heights of victory you have so longed to reach. Mount into them, then, with thankful hearts, and lose sight of all second causes in the shining of His love who will carry you in His arms safely and triumphantly over it all."* [4]

12. When a person responds with kindness instead of rudeness when she is mistreated, what is she evidencing in

her life? Read Galatians 5:16 and 22.

13. Why could kindness be called a "silent servant"? Read 1 Peter 3:1.

14. Describe how the following statement relates to kindness: "I would rather see a sermon than hear one any day."

"During the Korean War a chaplain saw a severely wounded soldier lying on the field of battle. Wanting to minister to him, he inquired, 'Would you like for me to read some strengthening passages from the Bible?'

'Right now I had rather have a drink. I'm dying of thirst,' was the reply.

And away rushed the chaplain who soon returned with water to quench the fallen soldier's thirst. Then he took off his scarf, rolled it into a little pillow, and placed it under the soldier's head.

'I'm so cold,' mumbled the badly wounded soldier.

On hearing this, the chaplain removed his top coat and spread it over the ill man.

'Now,' whispered the attended soldier, 'if there's anything in that book that makes you so kind, read it to me, please.' " [5]

A Biblical example of kindness is David's actions toward Mephibosheth. Read the account in 2 Samuel 9.

15. What had happened to Saul and Jonathan? Read
    1 Samuel 31:1–6.

16. What was David's motive in 2 Samuel 9?

17. Who was Mephibosheth, and what was wrong with him?
    Compare 2 Samuel 9:3 and 2 Samuel 4:4.

18. What things did David do for Mephibosheth?

19. Why do you think the Holy Spirit included this incident
    in the inspired Scripture?

20. How does Jesus look upon our acts of kindness? Read
    Matthew 25:35–40.

Many people in our world are helpless and hopeless,
some even homeless. Does someone in your community

need a meal or some clothes for their children? Ask God to lay some needy person on your heart, someone to whom you could show kindness. Ask God what you can do to help brighten this person's day—then do it!

"If we are never kind to others what good are we in the world? None! No good to self, no good to one's fellowman. Life is only a vain existence. However—

> *If by one word I help another,*
> *A struggling and despairing brother,*
> *Or ease one bed of pain;*
> *If I but aid some sad one weeping,*
> *Or comfort one, lone vigil keeping,*
> *I have not lived in vain."* [6]

♡ *From My Heart*

Recently I read a story that reminded me of this quotation by Ian Thomas: "God has a secret method by which He recompenses His saints: He sees to it that they become the prime beneficiaries of their own benefactions!"

The story was recorded in 1803. It told of a wealthy merchant who retired in a lovely home on the banks of a river. One cold, wintry morning, while still dressed in his chamber-robe, he walked onto his terrace, which was slightly elevated above the river. He saw a young man thrown from a furious horse into the swift currents of the river. Without stopping a moment to think about his own safety, he threw off his robe, jumped into the icy water, and swam to the other side. He brought the drowning stranger up just as he was about to lose consciousness. When he saw the man's face, he cried, "O God, what do I owe Thee? I have saved my son!"

When we give kindness, we'll receive kindness a thousand times over—and sometimes in strange and unusual ways.

"Lord, help me to practice kindness so regularly that it just becomes the natural thing to do."

"Let me be a little kinder, let me be a little blinder
To the faults of those about me; let me praise a
*   little more.*
Let me be a little meeker with the brother that is
*   weaker;*
Let me think more of my neighbor and a little less
*   of me."* [7]

From Your Heart

Plan to do some acts of kindness. You don't have to plan big things; little acts are appreciated too! Plan something for your family, something for a friend, and something for a stranger. The very doing of the deed brings its own reward!

Notes:
    1. De Jong, p. 209.
    2. A. C. A. Hall, quoted by Tileston, p. 332.
    3. Edward Meyrick Goulburn, quoted by Tileston, p. 206.
    4. Hannah Whitall Smith, quoted by Tileston, p. 272.
    5. Leroy Brownlow, *The Fruit of the Spirit* (Fort Worth: Brownlow Publishing Company, 1982, 1989), pp. 55, 56.
    6. Brownlow, pp. 53, 54.
    7. De Jong, p. 210.

Submit to One Another

"Submitting yourselves one to another in the fear of God"
(Ephesians 5:21).

Few women like the word "submit." Just the mention of the word makes them clench their fists, set their jaws, and curl their toes. We live in an age of independence and self-control. God's description of Israel in Judges 21:25 describes our generation as well, "Every man did that which was right in his own eyes." Today's baby-boomers' translation of that verse might be, "I'm going to do MY thing, MY way!" No wonder so few people feel happy and fulfilled. God said the way to fulfillment is through submission.

1. What does it mean to "submit"?

2. Read Ephesians 5:18–21. What three things will be evident in our lives when we are controlled by the Holy Spirit?
   Verse 19:

   Verse 20:

   Verse 21:

Only people who move from a self-controlled life to a Spirit-controlled life find fulfillment and satisfaction in submitting to one another.

3. Who is the supreme example of humble, obedient submission? Read Philippians 2:7 and 8.

"A surrendered heart—a heart totally dependent upon My grace—is the greatest gift you can offer Me. I realize your difficulty. . . . Trust me! Surrender all. Give Me room to act! What have you got to lose? Nothing but your vanity. Thankfully!" [1]

---

4. (a) What two kinds of mind are presented in Romans 8:5–9?

(b) Which mind is submissive?

Submission to God
5. Look up the word "sovereign" in the dictionary and write the definition here.

6. How do these verses describe God's sovereignty?
Psalm 115:3

Isaiah 14:27

Proverbs 16:9

Lamentations 3:37

7. When we realize that God is sovereign, how should we feel about submitting to Him?

"Learn to 'take' the yoke on you. Do not wait for it to be forced on you. Say, 'Yes, Lord,' to each expression of His will in all the circumstances of your lives. Say it with full consent to everything: to the loss of your health, to the malice of enemies, or to the cruelty of friends. Take each yoke as it comes, and in the taking you will find rest.

Notice the expressions 'I will give you rest' and 'ye shall find rest' in Matthew 11:28–29. This rest cannot be earned, bought, or attained. It is simply given by God and found by us. All who come to Christ in the way of surrender and trust 'find' it without any effort. They 'enter into rest' (cf. Heb. 4:3), for in His presence there is never any unrest." [2]

Submission in the Home

8. Read Ephesians 6:1–3 and Proverbs 3:1–4. Why should children submit to their parents?

9. Read Ephesians 5:21–28. What are the responsibilities of the wife and husband?

10. Why should a wife submit to her husband? Check each correct reason.

___ Because he is smarter.

___ Because God has given him the care and protection of the wife.

___ Because men are less emotional than women.

___ Because God has assigned her this responsibility.

11. What are the advantages of a wife's submitting to her husband? Read 1 Peter 3:1–4.

" 'We've been married a year and never quarreled. If a difference of opinion arises and I'm right, my husband gives in.'
    'And what if he's right?'
    'That has never occurred.' "[3]

Submission at Work

12. Read Ephesians 6:5–8. Paul wrote this to Christian slaves who probably had unsaved masters. If Paul were writing this today, what might he say?

13. If you have a difficult time submitting to your employer, what can you do instead of complaining? Read 1 Peter 5:5–7.

"Is there a situation in your life to which you need to return and submit? Has the Lord found you running away from something? Do you feel that you have been unfairly treated? Perhaps you have asked rebelliously, 'Why do I have to do that?' or 'Why can't I do what I want to do?' . . . The 'self way' never brings real peace and joy. Victory and power will come as we sweetly submit our wills and ways to God. This is not easy. Our wills are

strong. But great blessing comes in returning and submitting." [4]

Submission to the Government

14. How do we see God's sovereignty expressed in government? Read Daniel 4:17.

15. Why must we submit to national and civil authorities? Read Romans 13:1–7.

16. What are some practical ways in which we submit to the government?

Submission in the Church

17. What attitude should the pastor have toward the church members? Read 1 Peter 5:1–4.

18. What attitude should you have toward your pastor? Read 1 Thessalonians 5:12 and 13 and Hebrews 13:17.

19. What is the opposite of submission?

20. Which word describes your life: submission or resistance?

> Oh, break my life if need must be,
> No longer mine, I give it Thee.
> Oh, break my will; the off'ring take.
> For blessing comes when Thou dost break.[5]

♡ *From My Heart*

I remember the first time I had to submit to Christ. I say "had to" because I didn't want to! I had been resisting God's will in my life for five years. When God brought me to my knees, I was home alone. I vividly remember getting down on my knees in my dining room and saying, "Lord, You win, I lose! You're just too powerful; I can't fight against You any longer." That day I surrendered my will to do God's will and told Him I would do whatever He wanted me to do. I felt I was losing all my freedom and joy—only to find out I would enjoy freedom and joy such as I had never experienced before.

In the years since then, I've learned that living a consistent, victorious life filled with freedom and joy involves daily submission to Christ. The experience in my dining room was just the first step. The time you walked down the aisle in your church was just the beginning. Daily we must submit our wills to do God's will. I call it "palms-up" living.

Remember: God will not make us submit, but He can make us pretty miserable if we don't!

From Your Heart ♡

How do you react to the word "submit"? To whom do you have the hardest time submitting? What area of your life do you need to totally submit to God?

Notes:
1. Charles Slagle, *From the Father's Heart* (Shippensburg, PA: Destiny Image Publishers, 1989), p. 82.
2. Hannah Whitall Smith, quoted by Melvin E. Dieter and Hallie A. Dieter, editors, *God Is Enough* (Grand Rapids: Francis Asbury Press, 1986), p. 192.
3. Doan, p. 159.
4. Millie Stamm, *Meditation Moments* (Grand Rapids: Zondervan Publishing House, 1967), March 12.
5. Al Bryant, compiler, *Climbing the Heights* (Grand Rapids: Zondervan Publishing House, 1956), January 24.

Bear One Another's Burdens

"Bear ye one another's burdens, and so fulfil the law of Christ" (Galatians 6:2).

Galatians 6:2 commands us to bear one another's burdens. The word "burdens" refers to something so oppressive and weighty that it would cause the one carrying it to stumble and fall under the load. The burden may be the result of a circumstance beyond the bearer's control, his sin, or the sin of another. The result of the burden is usually the same: anxiety and turmoil. Continuing to carry the burden alone will increase the anxiety and keep the person from growing spiritually.

This command follows the description of the fruit of the Spirit in Galatians 5:22 and 23. Love, joy, peace, long-suffering, gentleness, goodness, faithfulness, meekness, and self-control cannot grow in an overburdened heart. The heavy burden of anxiety, grief, and guilt smothers peace. The weighty burden of resentment keeps us from enjoying love. The awful burden of anger robs us of long-suffering, gentleness, and goodness. The ugly burden of demanding answers for life's problems never allows us to develop meekness. The burden of selfishness steals the joys of faithfulness and self-control.

We must get free from these burdens, not just grit our teeth and learn to endure them. How do we get free from them? By learning to give them away. We must give them to the Lord and to others who are willing to help us bear them. Burden-bearing involves two people walking together, carrying the same load. We cannot bear another person's burden *for* her, but we can bear it *with* her.

Bear One Another's Burdens
Read Galatians 6:1–5.

1. Who needs someone to help her with her burden (v. 1)?

2. What do the words "overtaken in a fault" suggest?

3. What is the brother (or sister) in Christ admonished to do?

"The granting of restorative grace is among the greatest and most unique gifts one Christian can give another." [1]

---

4. Can just any Christian be a "restorer," or are there special qualifications?

5. Which fruit of the Spirit is highlighted in Galatians 6:1?

6. Define meekness.

"Meekness is the mark of a man who has been mastered by God." [2]

---

7. What does the word "restore" mean? Look up the meaning in a Bible dictionary.

8. A broken bone has to be set properly. Otherwise, it will not heal correctly and the person will continue to have problems. How does this relate to restoring a sister in the spirit of meekness?

9. What kind of spirit does a Christian have who looks at others who have fallen and says, "That could never happen to me"? Read Proverbs 16:18.

10. A person with a meek spirit will not be proud and arrogant; she will have a humble, submissive spirit. How will this humble spirit help her in her treatment of others? Read 1 Corinthians 10:12.

"If we wish to teach people who are walking in error, we cannot deal with them arrogantly. We may win the argument because we have the Word of God but lose people doing it. We need to instruct with meekness from the Scripture so they can see the error of their way." [3]

11. What is the warning in the last part of Galatians 6:1?

"When the body and the emotions and the mind are stretched to the limit, the risk of sinful choices climbs out of sight." [4]

12. What sure preventative can we use to keep us from sin? Read Psalm 119:11.

13. Why can't we take the attitude, "She made her bed; let her sleep in it"? Read Galatians 6:2.

> "Satan has achieved a real victory when he succeeds in getting us to react in an unspiritual way toward sins and failures in our brethren. We cannot fight sin with sin or draw men to God by frowning at them in fleshly anger, 'for the wrath of man worketh not the righteousness of God.' " [5]

14. According to Galatians 6:2, why should we bear one another's burdens?

15. What law are we fulfilling when we bear one another's burdens? Read John 13:34.

> " 'It is not enough,' said the ancient wise man, 'to say that you live your life so that you do not give any trouble to others. It would be a very good world indeed if all men could achieve that goal. But the vicissitudes of life are such that all men cannot, and some will be trouble to others in spite of their desires and hopes. That is why it is important for those who are more fortunate to be able to say, 'I also help others who have more trouble than they can handle alone.' " [6]

16. In Galatians 6:3 Paul reminded the believers to beware of pride. How can pride cause us to fall?

17. Why does pride like to expose another person's weakness? Read Galatians 6:4.

18. Who are we responsible to expose or examine according to verse 4?

What should we do for a sister who sins? Try to restore her—that's a part of bearing one another's burdens. Why should we do it? Because of love. How should we do it? In the "spirit of meekness," not with an arrogant spirit of condemnation.

19. Other than the burden of sin, what other burdens do people carry that we may be able to help bear?

20. What practical things can burden-bearers do?

"There came a time, after the immediate pain had subsided, that they [a couple whose child was divorced] took some initiative and asked certain friends why they were avoiding them. . . . People admitted they didn't realize that even a short prayer, a touch, or a hug when they met these friends in the church halls would have helped a great deal. A simple reminder that they weren't alone or disliked would have been a helpful gift. What the sufferer, in such encounters, needs to hear is that he or she is loved and surrounded by understanding." [7]

Bear Your Own Burden

Galatians 6:2 and 5 seem to contradict each other. After telling his readers to "bear ye one another's burdens," Paul wrote, "For every man shall bear his own burden." Paul used two different Greek words (the language in which he wrote) for "burden." The word in verse 2 means "a heavy burden"; the word in verse 5 describes "a soldier's pack." Each soldier is responsible to carry his own backpack. It could be illustrated like this.

Each believer must bear burdens or responsibilities that cannot be shared with others. The Lord reminds us that such burdens are light because He helps us share the load (Matthew 11:28–30). "Casting all your care [burdens] upon him; for he careth for you" (1 Peter 5:7).

Believers who learn to share their burdens with the Lord will have enough grace and strength to help bear the burdens of others.

From My Heart

Following the bombing of the federal building in Oklahoma City in 1995, the President spoke to the hurting people in that city. He said, "You will overcome this horror! You will rebuild, and we will be there to help you." When I heard that, I thought of struggling believers who fall into sin. They need to hear words like that from us. They need to know their life isn't over. They need to know God will forgive and we will forgive. With God's help, they can overcome this horror in their lives and rebuild. The question I must ask myself is, Will I be there to help?

Too often, our first reaction is disgust rather than the desire to help. We are like the Pharisees in John 8 who would rather condemn a fallen believer than help to restore him or her. This study helps us see the need to be tender-hearted when dealing with burdened people rather than hardhearted. Someone has said that a load is only half a load when two are carrying it. If we really care, there are burdens we can share!

From Your Heart

Whom do you know who is carrying a heavy burden right now? How can you help with that burden? Become a burden-bearer today!

Notes:

1. Gordon MacDonald, *Rebuilding Your Broken World* (Nashville: Thomas Nelson Publishers, 1988), p.182.

2. Geoffrey B. Wilson, quoted by John Blanchard, compiler, *Gathered Gold* (Durham, England: Evangelical Press, 1984), p. 201.

3. Robert C. Gage, *Cultivating Spiritual Fruit* (Schaumburg, IL: Regular Baptist Press, 1986), p. 118.

4. Gordon MacDonald, p. 117.

5. Tozer, quoted by Smith, November 27.

6. *Nuggets,* January 1961.

7. Gail MacDonald, *Keep Climbing* (Wheaton, IL: Tyndale House Publishers, 1989), pp.190, 191.

Honor One Another

"Be kindly affectioned one to another with brotherly love; in honour preferring one another" (Romans 12:10).

We all like to receive recognition. Something in us likes to be appreciated. Is this wrong? Yes and no! We should never seek recognition or honor; but if it is given in love, we should humbly receive it.

God's Word tells us to honor, or prefer, one another. What does that mean? It means we should not be so pre-occupied with our own plans, needs, goals, and wants that we cannot think of others. Our busy, overcrowded lives force us to dwell more and more on our needs instead of thinking how we can bless and give honor, or preference, to others.

Philippians 2:3 says, "Let nothing be done through strife or vainglory; but in lowliness of mind let each esteem other better than themselves." Esteem and appreciation are what we want; so let's give it to others. Let's not just do what they do for us (Luke 6:31); let's go one step further. Let's do *more* than they do for us! This means we need to change our focus from self to others. Instead of trying to receive honor and preference, let's try esteeming others better than ourselves. We may be amazed at what joy we will receive.

The Wrong Way to Give Honor

1. Read Romans 12:1–10. Write a summary of these verses.

2. Showing special preference or consideration for others should be done in a spirit of love without dissimulation (v. 9). What does "dissimulation" mean?

42

3. Give reasons why we might use empty flattery with each person listed.
   An employer

   An employer to an employee

   A wealthy relative

"Avoid flowery flatterers, for they can be robbers in disguise. Beneath the appealing mask there may be a manipulative exploiter ready to take advantage of an age-old weakness." [1]

---

4. What is the result of flattery? Read Proverbs 26:28.

5. How can people be ruined by flattery? Read Proverbs 16:18.

"When we need advice, the worst kind comes from a flatterer who gives us unfounded hopes and inflated visions. We need the facts, and only a true person will give them to us." [2]

---

6. Preferring others doesn't mean empty flattery, nor does it mean belittling ourselves. How do people belittle themselves?

7. How did Moses belittle himself? Read Exodus 4:10.

8. How did God rebuke Moses? Read Exodus 4:11 and 12.

"The way we continually talk about our own inability is an insult to the Creator. The deploring of our own incompetence is a slander against God for having overlooked us. Get into the habit of examining in the sight of God the things that sound humble before men, and you will be amazed at how staggeringly impertinent they are." [3]

---

9. Read 1 Timothy 5:21. What is the difference between preferring one another and preferring one before another?

Honoring, or preferring, one another does not mean giving empty flattery, belittling ourselves, or showing partiality. Let's see what it does mean.

The Right Way to Give Honor

The simplest way to explain "in honour preferring one another" is "putting others ahead of yourself."

10. What does "better" mean in Philippians 2:3?

11. What attitudes do we need in order to put others ahead of ourselves? Read Romans 12:10 and Philippians 2:5–7.

> *"How long is it going to take God to free us from the morbid habit of thinking about ourselves? We must get sick unto death of ourselves, until there is no longer any surprise at anything God can tell us about ourselves."* [4]

12. Give an illustration of how you can in honor prefer another person ahead of yourself.

> *"Someone may be given a place of service which you think you should occupy. In fact, you may even deserve it. Let us not be upset and concerned about such seeming injustices. Let us not become bitter when another receives the credit for what we have done. . . . 'A good violinist is one with the ability to play first fiddle and a willingness to play second.'"* [5]

13. How did Abraham illustrate "preferring one another" with his nephew Lot? Read Genesis 13:1–11.

14. Read John 3:29 and 30. How can we imitate John's attitude, "He [Christ] must increase, but I must decrease"?

> The world, I thought, belonged to me—
> Goods, gold and people, land and sea—
> Where'er I walked beneath God's sky
> In those old days my word was "I."
>
> Years passed; there flashed my pathway near
> The fragment of a vision dear;
> My former word no more sufficed,
> And what I said was—"I and Christ."

> But, O, the more I looked on Him,
> His glory grew, while mine grew dim,
> I shrank so small, He towered so high,
> All I dared say was—"Christ and I."
>
> Years more the vision held its place
> And looked me steadily in the face;
> I speak now in humbler tone,
> And what I say is—"Christ alone." [6]

15. Why should we honor, or esteem, our spiritual leaders? Read 1 Thessalonians 5:12 and 13 and Hebrews 13:17.

We live in a reward-seeking society. If we are not careful, it will influence our thinking. What does the Bible say about rewards?

16. Read 1 Corinthians 3:10–14 and 2 Corinthians 5:10. When will Christians receive rewards?

17. Are God's rewards based on quality of work or quantity of work? Why?

18. How can 1 Corinthians 3:14 encourage a person who has faithfully served God for many years without honor or recognition?

If you are building with wood, hay, and stubble for the praise and honor of men, enjoy it while it lasts, because that will be the only honor you receive. You won't hear any words of praise and honor from Christ. If, however, you are serving God faithfully with pure motives, you will hear His "well done, thou good and faithful servant . . . enter thou into the joy of thy lord" (Matthew 25:21).

From My Heart

Over the years as a pastor's wife and now as a pastor's wife and author, I have received much honor and praise. It has been more than I deserve, but it has been appreciated. I can honestly say the only honor I have ever sought is the honor of being a vessel the Master could use. "But in a great house there are not only vessels of gold and of silver, but also of wood and of earth; and some to honour, and some to dishonour. If a man therefore purge himself from these, he shall be a vessel unto honour, sanctified, and meet for the master's use, and prepared unto every good work" (2 Timothy 2:20, 21).

How about you? Do you want to be a clay pot or a gold pot? We can all receive honor from Christ. Romans 2:10 says, "But glory, honour, and peace, to every man that worketh good." The greater the good work, the greater the honor. But remember—only that which is done for God's glory and in His power will be honored by Him!

From Your Heart

Are you ever guilty of empty flattery? Maybe you have a problem with belittling yourself. How can you Biblically carry out the command to honor others? Think of someone you know who deserves to be honored for his or her service for Christ. Let that person know how much you appreciate his or her ministry.

Notes:

1. *Thoughts of Gold* (Fort Worth: Brownlow Publishing Co., 1974, 1990), p. 36.

2. *Thoughts of Gold,* p. 36.

3. Chambers, p. 335.

4. Chambers, p. 173.

5. Stamm, March 29.

6. Mrs. Charles E. Cowman, *Streams in the Desert—2* (Grand Rapids: Zondervan Publishing House, 1966), p. 144.

LESSON 7

Comfort One Another

"Wherefore comfort one another with these words"
(1 Thessalonians 4:18).

One Sunday my husband shared with our congregation that one of our mothers had just found out her teenager was on drugs and would have to go to a rehabilitation center. Then he announced that three elderly women were in a car accident; one was killed and two were severely injured. Here were four families that needed comfort—not only from God, but also from friends and loved ones.

We're living in a world of helpless and hopeless people who shout, "I can't take it anymore!" Headlines in our newspapers scream of murder and crime, the AIDS epidemic, and soon-to-be-insufficient Social Security benefits. As our clocks tick away, like time bombs ready to explode, people feel less and less secure about anything or anyone in this wicked world.

Into such a world of hopelessness, God calls His children to comfort one another: "Wherefore comfort one another with these words" (1 Thessalonians 4:18). With what words? Words of hope. Jesus is coming again, and all our trials and pains will cease. And best of all, we'll see Jesus and all our loved ones who have gone to Heaven before us.

If we did not have God's Word, we would have no message of hope to comfort this hopeless generation or one another.

Are you willing to be a comforter? It will cost you time, energy, and a wounded heart. Stanley Jones, a medical missionary in India, once said, "When you comfort others, you are in danger of getting the plague of that person's sadness or pain on your heart." It's a risk—but the gain is worth the pain!

The Basis for Our Message of Comfort and Hope

1. What must you know before you can comfort others? Read 2 Corinthians 1:3 and 4.

2. Second Corinthians 1:3 calls our Father in Heaven the "God of all comfort." How significant is the word "all" in this verse?

3. Considering what you learned in questions 1 and 2, what is the basis of the message of comfort?

> *"The Bible is a great treasury of reserved blessing. ... The light, the comfort, the help are all there, but we do not see it. We cannot see it until we have a fuller sense of need. The rich truths seem to be hiding away, refusing to disclose their meaning. When we begin to experience the struggles, trials, and conflicts of real life, then the new senses begin to reveal themselves in the old familiar sentences. Promises that seemed as if they were written in invisible ink now begin to glow with rich meaning, flash out like newly lighted lamps, and pour bright beams upon the path of life."* [1]

4. Look up the following verses. Explain how each verse conveys a message of comfort and hope.
   Isaiah 66:13

2 Corinthians 7:6

John 14:16

Isaiah 49:16

Romans 15:4

"Divine comfort does not come to us in any mysterious or arbitrary way. It comes as the result of a divine method. The indwelling Comforter 'brings to our remembrance' comforting things concerning our Lord, and, if we believe them, we are comforted by them." [2]

The Basis for Being a Comforter
Your life must display a message of hope.

5. What must be real and vital in your life before you can give a message of comfort and hope to others? Read Philippians 4:4 and 11.

". . . Although He declares Himself to be the God of all comfort, they [some Christians] continually complain that they cannot find comfort anywhere; and their sorrowful looks and the doleful tones of their voice show that they are speaking the truth.

Such Christians, although they profess to be followers of the God of all comfort, spread gloom and discomfort around them wherever they go;

and it is out of the question for them to hope that they can induce anyone else to believe that this beautiful name, by which He has announced Himself, is anything more than a pious phrase, which in reality means nothing at all."[3]

Your comfort must come from God's Word.

6. Why is God's Word more important than a psychology book or a best-selling recovery book? Read Romans 15:4.

You must receive God's comfort before you can give it.

7. Read Job 5:7 and 14:1. What do we all experience in this life? How can this help us comfort others?

You must identify with another person's hurt.

8. What is the difference between sympathy and empathy?

9. Do you have to suffer the same experience to identify with another person's pain?

"The power to console lies not in our ability to use a particular formula that shall suit a particular want: it lies in our acquaintance with God and His ways and the quickness of our sympathies with

> *men. No one whose heart is tender and whose faith is strong may be deterred from trying to console a sufferer because he has not experienced a like calamity. The experience which is so valuable in all contact with souls is a tone of spirit rather than a knowledge of details; and it is this which is God's choice gift to those He comforts.*"[4]

10. Why is a person who has experienced much heartache and pain usually a good comforter?

You must be alert to the feelings that lie beneath the words.

11. Read Job 7:11. Why must we not be surprised or judgmental when the hurting person is angry or full of complaint?

Verses of Comfort to Share with Hurting People

12. In what situations or circumstances would each of these verses give comfort?
    Psalm 23:4

    Psalm 27:1

    Hebrews 13:5

    Psalm 27:10

Philippians 4:19

Psalm 69:20 and 33

13. What other verses have you used in comforting others or yourself?

"The psalmist says, 'In the multitude of my thoughts within me thy comforts delight my soul.' But I am afraid that among the multitude of our thoughts within us there are far too often many more thoughts of our own discomforts than of God's comforts. We must think of His comforts if we are to be comforted by them. It might be a good exercise of soul for some of us to analyze our thoughts for a few days, and see how many thoughts we actually do give to God's comforts, compared with the number we give to our own discomforts. I think the result would amaze us!" [5]

Comforting Thoughts about Our God of All Comfort

14. When you are distressed and full of anxiety, think about the greatness of God. Look up the verses below and fill in the blanks.

Psalm 3:3—He is my_____.

Psalm 40:17—He is my _____ and

_____.

Matthew 6:9—He is my _____.

Isaiah 9:6—He is my wonderful _____ .

Psalm 91:2—He is my _____ and

_____.

Psalm 71:3—He is my _____ and

_____.

Now Comfort One Another

15. What is the most important thing you can do to be a good comforter? Read 2 Timothy 2:15.

16. When you don't have any answers, but you want to comfort your hurting friend, what can you do? Read Job 2:11–13.

"We first discovered the role of the comforter-friend many years ago when our daughter Kris, then two years old, accidently drank some turpentine and was rushed to the hospital gasping for air.

... Though that memory is twenty years old, both of us vividly recall the men and women who, as comforter-friends, came and sat with us. A prayer, an embrace, a cup of coffee, silence when necessary. They simply sat with us, sharing our pain. No answers or explanations were offered because there were none to give." [6]

"God does not comfort us to make us comfortable, but to make us comforters." Who needs your comfort? Are you willing to pay the price? Remember: the gain is worth the pain!

From My Heart

Someone once told me, "A mother is only as happy as her unhappiest child." One of my sons is going through a difficult experience, and my husband and I are feeling the pain and heartache with him. A young mother, who is going through a hurtful experience herself, gave me a gift to comfort and encourage me. She was at my Bible study when I asked the ladies to pray for my son. She gave me a little basket with a 3 x 5 card in it, a card of encouragement, and seven other items. The 3 x 5 card read as follows:

1. The cellophane tape is to remind you that a broken heart can be mended by God.
2. The little bottle is to collect your tears (Psalm 56:8).
3. The hanky is to remind you that someone else needs you to dry her tears with a few words or a note.
4. The card is to show that I care.
5. The little scissors are to cut out all unnecessary stuff that causes you a lot of stress.
6. The nail is to remind you that Christ coped with a heavy load of stress for us.
7. The thumbtack is to remind you not to just sit on your problems.
8. The chalk is to remind you that when something undesirable happens you can just chalk it up to experience.

Thank you, Sally, for being a comforter-friend! Her comfort and encouragement to me reminded me again of the value of comforters.

It's great to have the Comforter living in me and the God of all comfort in Heaven and Jesus Christ, Who sticks closer than a brother, at my side; but it is also good to have a comforter with flesh and bones who can hug me now and then.

"Lord, let my mouth speak words of comfort. Let my arms be used to comfort. Let my hands write notes of comfort. Lord, let me take time to be a comforter-friend!"

From Your Heart

Do you have a comforter-friend? Have you ever thanked her for just being there for you? To whom can you be a comforter-friend?

Notes:

1. Cowman, *Streams—2*, p. 225.

2. Hannah Whitall Smith, *The God of All Comfort* (Chicago: Moody Press, 1956), p. 42.

3. Smith, *The God of All Comfort*, p. 32.

4. A. Mackennal, quoted by James Comper Gray and George M. Adams, *Gray & Adams Bible Commentary*, vol 5: Romans—Revelation (Grand Rapids: Zondervan Publishing House), p. 181.

5. Smith, *The God of All Comfort*, p. 46.

6. Gail MacDonald, p. 191.

Show Hospitality to One Another

"Use hospitality one to another without grudging"
(1 Peter 4:9).

The pastor gives the closing prayer, and the people file out the doors. They hurry to their cars and go home. When is the last time you invited someone home with you after the morning or evening service for a meal or just a time of felowship? During the church service, we may deepen our fellowship with God, but there is little time to deepen our fellowship and relationships with other believers. For this to happen, we need to get together in one another's homes.

One of the requirements for being a pastor is that he be "given to hospitality" (1 Timothy 3:2) and "a lover of hospitality" (Titus 1:8) As the pastor's wife, I realize my husband can't carry out that responsibility without my help. It is not always easy; in fact, it never is; but I do my best to have groups in our home for times of fellowship. We try to invite several new couples along with some of our regulars for get-acquainted times. We also have missionaries and other speakers occasionally. I want our church to be a friendly church where people are having one another in their homes, so I must set the example for them. Many of us find it easier to take people to a restaurant than to have them in our homes. Does it make a difference? Is hospitality really that important? Let's find out what God's Word has to say.

1. What is hospitality? Look up the definition in the dictionary.

2. How did Christ plan for His disciples' care? Read Matthew 10:9–14.

3. How did Christ equate hospitable treatment of His disciples with treatment of Himself? Read Matthew 25:40.

"Hospitality should have no other nature than love." [1]

Hospitality Most Often Involves a Home

4. The Bible mentions three types of people to whom we are to open our homes. Who are they? Read Proverbs 31:20, Hebrews 13:2, and 1 Peter 4:9 and 10.

5. Who would be a "needy person" or a "stranger" whom you might have in your home?

6. What can we learn from the example of Lydia? Read Acts 16:14, 15, and 40.

7. Why should we have other believers in our homes? Read 1 Peter 4:8–10.

". . . The church is filled with strangers who have known each other for years. What a contradiction to Christian fellowship! God wants his people loving one another past the superficial exchanges strangers give. . . . Hospitality is an investment of quality time in which we're used of God to meet another's need." [2]

---

8. What people do we tend to shun and probably never think of inviting to our homes?

9. Is it wise to have only "our kind of people" in our homes? Why or why not? Read Hebrews 13:2.

10. Some people never have other people in their homes. Why do you think this is?

One of the most often used excuses for not having people in our homes is, "Oh, my house is a mess; I don't have time to get it ready for company." I've used that excuse myself. Whenever I think my house is a mess, I realize it could be worse. I enjoy this poem from *Sidetracked Home Executives—From Pigpen to Paradise.*

The Housewife

There was a housewife I once knew
Who had so much work that she wanted to do.
She had eight loads of laundry to wash and to dry,
Five beds to make and groceries to buy.
Library books three years overdue,
She thought, "Go to the library? No, let's go to the
      zoo."
"Hurray!" cried her children. But, alas, they stayed
      home.
The eight loads of laundry had all the clothes that
      they owned.
She had dishes from dinner the night before
And gum to scrape off the kitchen floor.
And just as she knelt to scrape up the gum,
She thought about popcorn and she wanted some.
So she got out the popper; it was full of rice.
And she thought to herself, "It would be nice
To get out the pictures of my wedding dress,"
But she couldn't find them because of the mess
In her living room where she kept a shelf
Full of books on how to improve herself.
So she picked out a book and she sat and she read.
And she thought to herself, "I'll take a nap instead."
So she stretched and she yawned and flopped into
      bed.
Then she remembered something her husband had
      said.
So she got out the iron and she looked for his shirt
Which had fallen into a pile of dirt
She had swept in a corner a few days before
And had stopped because someone had knocked at
      the door.
Then she sighed, "Oh dear!" and she moaned, "Poor
      me!"
And she grabbed a sack of taco chips and turned on
      the TV.
She watched all the game shows.
And she watched "Love of Life."
And she dreamed of becoming the perfect wife! [3]

11. Is there a difference between entertaining and
    hospitality?

"The purpose of hospitality is to deepen relationships, to meet needs. . . . Hospitality may take the form of a meal, an evening discussion. . . . It may mean a bed, some clothes, some money, or even a shoulder to cry on. Always, though, hospitality means sharing you." [4]

12. What kind of attitude does a good hostess have? Read 1 Peter 4:9.

13. What is another characteristic of a good hostess? Read Matthew 7:12.

14. How does God feel about our ministry to other believers? Read Hebrews 6:10.

15. If you haven't been sharing your home with others, what are you missing? Read Acts 20:35.

"The labor of baking was the hardest part of the sacrifice of her hospitality. To many it is easy to give what they have, but the offering of weariness and pain is never easy [George MacDonald, speaking about his wife]." [5]

16. Write down a few things you have enjoyed when you

have been a guest in someone's home. What made you really feel at home?

17. Planning ahead takes some of the stress out of hospitality. Why is this important?

Helpful Hints for Hostesses

I am not what you would call "the hostess with the mostest." Hospitality does not come easily for me. I had to learn to do this, and I also had to learn to like it! We can all learn to obey the command to show hospitality. Based on things I do when I have a food-and-fellowship gathering at our home, here are some suggestions for you:

• Invite as many people as your largest room will hold. Invite young couples, older couples, and singles. When you have a large group, you don't have to worry about lulls in the conversation. At these kinds of fellowships, we don't invite the children; otherwise the parents are occupied with their children and are not getting acquainted with other adults.

• Plan a get-acquainted or ice-breaker activity to get started. We like this activity: Have each person give his name, occupation, something about his family, and how long he has been attending the church. After each person gives his name, have him name a food or animal that starts with the first letter of his name; e.g., Juanita —Jello. Have the next person say "Juanita—Jello, and I'm Paul—Pear." The next person says, "Juanita—Jello, Paul—Pear, and I'm Sally—Salad." Continue around the room, having each person add a name to the list.

• Play a few group games so no one is put on the spot. We play Outburst, Bible Trivia, Scattergories, and similar games.

• Serve light refreshments, dessert, punch and coffee, or a vegetable tray and dessert tray. If your finances are limited, ask your guests to bring a dessert; call the get-together a "Dessert Smorgasbord." You may want to provide a vegetable tray for those on special diets.

Here are some of my favorite recipes.

Vegetable Pizza

Crust—2 cans Pillsbury Crescent Rolls. Pinch the squares together on a cookie sheet and bake as directed until brown. Cool.

Mix together and spread on crust: 2 8 oz. packages of cream cheese; 1 envelope of ranch dressing mix; 1 cup of Miracle Whip salad dressing.

Chop into small pieces and put on top: $3/4$ cup each—green onion, carrots, cauliflower, and broccoli. Press down.

Cover with foil and refrigerate overnight.

Top with 8 oz. package of shredded cheddar cheese just before serving.

Mint Brownies

Beat together:
- 1 cup sugar
- $1/2$ cup margarine
- 4 eggs

Add:
- 1 cup flour
- 1 16 oz. can chocolate syrup
- 1 tsp. vanilla

Put in greased 8 x 10 dish; bake 35 minutes in 350° oven. (Bake a 9 x 12 pan for 30 minutes.) Cool before frosting.

Frosting

Mix together:
- 2 cups powdered sugar
- $1/2$ cup margarine
- 2 tbs. milk
- $1/2$ tsp. peppermint extract

Frost cooled cake.

Chocolate Glaze

Melt 1 cup of chocolate chips and 6 tbs. of margarine for $3/4$ minute in microwave; stir. Pour over the frosting.

Slush Punch

Dissolve in a gallon container:

1 package strawberry Jello and 2 cups boiling water

Add:

2 cups sugar

1 package dry orange drink mix

1 can unsweetened pineapple juice

6 tbs. lemon juice

Stir. Add enough water to fill the container, leaving a little room at the top for expansion. Cover and put in the freezer. Allow 8 hours to freeze. Make in the evening. Stir in the morning. Set out 3 hours before serving.

Can you remember the last person you had in your home other than family? Now you know why you should have the needy, strangers, and believers in your home—and you know how you can do it. When will you do it?

"No duty, however hard and perilous, should be feared one-half so much as failure in the duty. People sometimes shrink from responsibility, saying they dare not accept it because it is so great. . . . We have abundant assurance that we shall receive all the strength we need to perform any duty God allots to us." [6]

♡ *From My Heart*

Becoming a pastor's wife was a giant step of faith for me and has continued to stretch my faith throughout the years. One of the most difficult tasks was opening my home to others. In the early years of our marriage, I often felt my house wasn't nice enough or clean enough. I felt I could not cook good enough to invite people to our home. Over the years I have learned God isn't concerned that I "show off" what I have but that I "share" what I have. I'm still not the world's greatest housekeeper or cook, but I don't let it bother me like it once did. I really try to enjoy having people in my home, not only for the benefit I receive from it but because I want to be obedient to Christ.

My husband loves to have people in our home, but he knows it is not an easy thing for me. He has learned to help me when we're having guests. I know that if I am really behind, he'll vacuum or do whatever I need. This has taken much of the pressure off me and has been a great encouragement to do more.

You know, those verses in 1 Timothy and Titus on "given to hospitality" and "a lover of hospitality" are written to the pastor. He should have been doing this all the time! Why didn't I think of that years ago? But look at all the blessings I would have missed if I hadn't done my part!

From Your Heart

Do you regularly have other believers in your home? If not, why not? What is your biggest fear in having guests in your home? Think of someone to invite and set a date. Start planning now!

Notes:
1. Henrietta Mears, quoted by Doan, p. 127.
2. Jim Phillips, *One Another* (Nashville: Broadman Press, 1981), p. 90.
3. Pam Young and Peggy Jones, *Sidetracked Home Executives* (New York: Warner Books, 1981), pp. 6, 7.
4. Phillips, pp. 90, 91.
5. George MacDonald, quoted by Tileston, p. 7.
6. J. R. Miller, quoted by Tileston, p. 323.

Lie Not One to Another

"Lie not one to another, seeing that ye have put off the old man with his deeds" (Colossians 3:9).

We live in a world of lying people. Politicians lie about one another. The mechanic lies about the parts he charged you for that he didn't replace. Parents ask their children to lie: "Tell them I'm not home." Couples lie to one another: they promise to live together until death, but they don't. Yes, lying is a common practice among the people of this world, and, unfortunately, even among Christians.

How does God feel about lying? How do you feel about lying? How can we help one another break the cycle of lying? We need to correct this miserable sin in our own lives before we try to help one another.

I once read that you need a good memory if you lie because it is easy to tell one lie but not easy to tell *just* one lie. The more you tell, the more you have to remember what you said last. "What a tangled web we weave / When first we practice to deceive."

The Root of Lying

1. What is a lie?

2. Why do children lie without being taught to do so? Read Romans 5:12 and Colossians 3:9.

3. How did lying originate? Read John 8:44.

66

4. What is God's relationship to lying? Read Hebrews 6:18.

5. What was Satan's first recorded lie? Read Genesis 3:1–6.

6. How do we copy this trick of Satan?

"Mrs. Brown was shocked to learn that Junior had told a lie. Taking the youngster aside for a heart-to-heart talk, she graphically explained the consequences of falsehood:

'A . . . man with red fiery eyes and two sharp horns grabs little boys who tell lies and carries them off at night. He takes them to Mars where they have to work in a dark canyon for fifty years. Now,' she concluded, satisfied, 'you won't tell a lie again, will you, dear?'

'No, Mom,' replied Junior gravely. 'You tell better ones.' " [1]

Lying is from the Devil. He started it, and he wants to keep it going. When we lie to one another, we are helping Satan carry out his mission on earth. Christians should be people of honesty and integrity. We are to be different from the rest of the world. We are to be beacons of truth in a dark, dishonest world.

Kinds of Lies
Deliberate lies

7. What is one reason people deliberately lie? Read Genesis 4:8 and 9.

"Four high school boys were late to their morning classes one day. They entered the classroom and solemnly told their teacher they were detained due to a flat tire. The sympathetic teacher smiled and told them it was too bad they were late because they had missed a test that morning. But she was willing to let them make it up. She gave them each a piece of paper and a pencil and sent them to four corners of the room. Then she told them they would pass if they could answer just one question: Which tire was flat?" [2]

---

8. Read Acts 5:1–11. (a) What was Ananias and Sapphira's lie?

(b) Why do you think they lied in this situation?

Half-truths or white lies

9. How did Abraham tell a half-truth? What important truth did he omit? Read Genesis 20:2, 3, and 12.

10. Why are half-truths so deceptive?

"How easy it is to be less than truthful, even for religious people. There are subtle as well as

salient perversions of truth, such as in the follow-ing sampling:

> *exaggerations to make an impression;*
> *twisting the truth in an appeal for funds;*
> *taking credit for what we have not earned;*
> *submitting inaccurate financial records;*
> *misrepresenting goods for sale;*
> *false excuses for absence, lateness or duties*
> *undone;*
> *cheating on an exam."* [3]

False witness

11. How does God feel about this kind of lying? Read Prov-erbs 6:16–19.

12. In Whose trial were false witnesses especially heinous? Read Matthew 26:57–64.

Gossip

13. A gossip spreads stories that may or may not be true about another person. How can gossip be the same as lying?

". . . We should ask five questions before listening to a carrier of an evil report:

1. What is your reason for telling me? Widen-ing the circle of gossip only compounds the prob-lem.

2. Where did you get your information? Re-fusal to identify the source of information is a sure sign of an evil report.

3. Have you gone to those directly involved? Spirituality is not measured by how well we expose an offender but by how effectively we restore an offender (Gal. 6:1). . . .

4. Have you personally checked out all of the facts? Even facts become distorted when not balanced with other facts or when given with negative motives.

5. Can I quote you if I check this out?" [4]

14. How should we respond if someone is telling lies and gossiping about us? Read 1 Peter 2:19–23.

"Among tribes ignorant of the methods of civilized warfare we find weapons which are little better than slim rods, and, although their points are sharp and poisoned, yet they proclaim their weakness when they come into collision with an experienced swordsman. Lying is such a weapon, and its use reveals the utter folly of him who wields it. It can no more stand against truth than the wooden spear of a savage can turn aside the thrust of a Damascus blade." [5]

Deceit

15. How did Jacob and Rebekah deceive Issac? Read Genesis 27:1–41.

16. How do some women use deceit and manipulation with their mates?

Exaggeration

17. If a person constantly exaggerates the truth, what sin is she demonstrating to others? Read Proverbs 27:2.

"A woman approached evangelist Billy Sunday after one of his sermons and asked pensively, 'I wonder if you can help me? I have a terrible habit of exaggeration.'

'Certainly, madam,' replied Sunday. 'Just call it lying!' " [6]

Hypocrisy

18. Why did Christ call the scribes and Pharisees hypocrites? Read Matthew 15:8 and 9.

19. Where are Christians most likely to practice hypocrisy?

"A little boy asked his mother, 'Mommy, what is a lie?' His mother answered by saying, 'Son, a lie is an abomination unto the Lord . . . but a very present help in time of need!'

Sad to say too often we teach a similar pattern to our children. Let's be careful to model clearly what we teach with our lips." [7]

Promise-breaking

20. What did Peter promise the Lord? Read Matthew 26:33–35.

21. What promise do married couples break today? Read Genesis 2:24 and Matthew 19:6.

Each time my husband performs a wedding ceremony, I think, "Does this couple really know what they are promising God and each other? Will they keep those promises?" I have written an Anniversary Prayer that I give a bride-to-be at her bridal shower. I encourage the couple to read this prayer each year on their anniversary to remind themselves of the vows they made before God and to each other.

The Results of Lying

22. List the end results of lying to God and others.
    Proverbs 20:17

    Proverbs 19:5

    Hebrews 12:6

How to Make Sure You Always Tell the Truth

- Admit that lying is sin (Proverbs 6:16, 17).
- Think before you speak (Proverbs 13:3).
- Talk less; keep silent (Proverbs 11:12).
- Weigh the consequences (Proverbs 19:9).
- Confess lying immediately (Proverbs 28:13).

23. If you have been caught in the vicious cycle of lying, how can you stop? Read Colossians 3:5–10 and Galatians 5:16 and 17.

From My Heart

I have been reminded over and over in the preparation of this lesson that God hates lying. He mentions lying twice in the lists of the seven sins that are an abomination to Him (Proverbs 6:16–19). He mentions it in the Ten Commandments (Exodus 20:16). Yes, God hates lying!

Why does God hate lying so much? I believe one of the main reasons is because it destroys our ability to put confidence in truth. Our whole relationship with God is built on truth, our belief in it and our response to it. A liar has great difficulty believing God. Therefore, he forfeits a multitude of blessings from God (Hebrews 11:6).

Why do Christians lie? To gain protection and advantage and to promote their own personal interests. I know professing Christians who have lied to get rich, to escape punishment, and to protect their reputation. Why do Christians lie? Because we are sinful and selfish! We may do it unintentionally, but all of us lie, and probably more frequently than we even realize. It is just an automatic result of our old sin nature. We need to ask God to make us miserable every time we lie.

I want God to prick my conscience and make me miserable. If I'm not miserable when I lie, it could get to be a habit, and eventually I won't even feel bad. A proverb says, "Conscience is a three-pointed thing in my heart that turns around when I do something wrong, and the points hurt. If I keep doing bad, the points wear off, and then it hurts no more."

"Lord, keep pricking my conscience and making me miserable when I tell those little white lies that are big black lies to You."

From Your Heart

When do you have the biggest problem with lying? Have you felt justified in telling half-truths or white lies? Do you still feel there are times when it is okay? Ask God to make you miserable anytime you are less than 100 percent truthful.

Notes:
  1. Doan, p. 145.
  2. Paul Harvey, quoted in "Selected Illustrations from *Bible Illustrator*" (Parsons Technology, Inc., 1990–91).
  3. Henry Gariepy, *Portraits of Perseverance* (Wheaton, IL: Victor Books, 1989), p. 159.
  4. "Selected Illustrations from *Bible Illustrator*."
  5. W. Harris, quoted by Gray and Adams, vol. 2: Chronicles—Proverbs, p. 798.
  6. Doan, p. 97.
  7. "Selected Illustrations from *Bible Illustrator*."

Wash One Another's Feet

*"If I then, your Lord and Master, have washed your feet; ye
also ought to wash one another's feet" (John 13:14).*

Words are cheap. It is easy to say "I love you"; it is
quite another thing to show it by our actions. One evidence
of Christian love is to wash one another's feet. If you have
never read John 13:1–17, you may be saying, "Get real!
Christ surely didn't mean we're really supposed to get down
and wash one another's feet." Some churches practice foot
washing during their communion services. However, the
lesson the Lord Jesus was teaching was broader than that.
Let's look at the passage.

The setting for John 13:1–17 was the evening before the
Passover Feast. Jesus was with the twelve disciples. They
were having their last supper together before Judas's betrayal of Jesus and His crucifixion. While the meal was being
served, Jesus taught these men a lesson that would change
their lives. It can be life-changing for us as well if we learn
and apply the lesson He taught.

The Example of Humility

1. Read John 13:1–4. Use a study Bible or Bible handbook
   to discover why it was a common practice in Bible times
   for a host to make sure his guests' feet were washed.

2. Who normally washed the guest's feet? Read 1 Samuel
   25:41.

3. What is the significance of the words in verse 3, "the Father had given all things into his hands" and verse 4, "and took a towel"?

"Humility comes when we realize God has given us everything. We don't have to pretend. We don't have to act as though we are important. We don't have to tell people how big we are—we have everything. 'All things are your's' [sic] (I Cor. 3:21). Everything has been put in our hands through Jesus Christ. . . .

When you realize this great truth, you can reach out, take up a towel and serve other people." [1]

---

4. Read John 13:5. What position would Jesus have been in to wash the disciples' feet?

"Something in my nature does not want to get down before anybody else and be a servant. And yet Jesus tells us that the happiest life is the life of service." [2]

---

5. Read John 13:6 and 7. The disciples didn't understand what Jesus was doing. He said they would understand "hereafter." What had to happen before they would understand? Compare John 13:1 and 2 with John 18:1, 2, 28; 19:1–6, 17, 18.

6. Describe a time in your life when you didn't understand what God was trying to teach you, but later it made sense.

> I do not know, I cannot see,
> What God's kind hand prepares for me,
> Nor can my glance pierce through the haze
> Which covers all my future ways;
> But yet I know that o'er it all
> Rules He who notes the sparrow's fall. [3]

7. Read John 13:8–11. Jesus told the disciples that a person who has already bathed needs to wash only his feet; the rest of his body is clean. What was the spiritual application He was making? Read Revelation 1:5, Titus 3:5, and 1 John 1:7–9.

8. Read John 13:12–14. Jesus knew the disciples didn't understand what He was doing, so He explained His actions. What did He tell them?

9. Read John 13:15–17. Was Jesus teaching the disciples they literally should wash each other's feet? If not, what was He teaching them?

> *"The real test of the saint is not preaching the gospel, but washing disciples' feet, that is, doing the things that do not count in the actual estimate of men but count everything in the estimate of God. . . . Paul focuses Jesus Christ's idea of a New Testament saint in his life, viz.: not one who proclaims the Gospel merely, but one who becomes broken bread and poured out wine in the hands of Jesus Christ for other lives."* [4]

10. How does Philippians 2:5–8 relate to John 13:1–17?

The Practice of Humility

11. Read Luke 22:19–30. John 13:1–7 and Luke 22:1–38 both describe the Last Supper. What kind of spirit was in the disciples' hearts?

12. How was Jesus' unforgettable object lesson a rebuke to the disciples?

> *"Pride is a vice which cleaveth so fast unto the hearts of men, that if we were to strip ourselves of all faults, one by one, we should undoubtedly find it the very last and hardest to put off."* [5]

13. What does it mean for us to follow Christ's example and wash one another's feet?

"Yes, God can reach His hand down from the heavens and touch a life. . . . He uses those who are the nearest by to lend a helping hand, to comfort, to lift from despair, to stroke the fevered brow of discontent. For how can that discouraged and fretful soul experience the love of God except through the love of one who is beside him ready to love. . . . It may be a friend or a stranger, but God uses hands which are consecrated to Him for touching lives." [6]

---

14. As a missionary was packing his barrels to go to the mission field, the pastor said, "Don't forget your towel!" Why do you think he said that? Read John 13:3–5 again.

15. If a "Humble Servant" award were to be given to someone in your church, whom would you nominate? Why?

16. Some people love to do and give for others, but is it possible to serve for the wrong reasons? What are some wrong reasons? Read Matthew 6:1 and 2.

The Secret of Humility
17. How can we learn to have a servant spirit? Read Philippians 2:3–5.

18. Read Philippians 2:3 and 4. Why do you think Christians do not regularly practice the equivalent of foot washing in their relationships with one another in the church? Check the appropriate answers:

___ We are too proud to humble ourselves and serve others.

___ We don't want to get too close to others.

___ We are overwhelmed with our own problems.

___ We are confused about how to get started.

___ We are too busy with our own agenda.

19. Some ladies serve outside their homes more than they serve their own families. How could we practice foot washing in our family relationships?

20. Has anyone ever demonstrated to you what it means to "wash one another's feet?" Describe the experience. Have you ever thanked the person?

21. How does true humility grow in our lives? Read Philippians 3:10.

"The mainspring of Paul's service is not love for men, but love for Jesus Christ. If we are devoted to the cause of humanity, we shall soon be crushed and broken-hearted, for we shall often meet with more ingratitude from men than we would from a dog; but if our motive is love to God, no ingratitude can hinder us from serving our fellow men." [7]

From My Heart

Augustine wisely said, "That which first overcame man is the last thing he overcomes." Of all the sins that corrupt me none is more wicked than pride! A humble, serving spirit is what I am striving for, but I still see pride's ugly head appearing too often. It seems like an oddity in the structure of things that pride—striving to be exalted—humiliates us, and humility—where we purposely are willing to be humiliated—is exalting; but that is God's plan.

The Lord "giveth grace unto the humble," and if you will "humble yourselves in the sight of the Lord, . . . he shall lift you up" (James 4:6, 10). The Lord gives grace to make us humble and keep us humble. He honors the humble with grace and glory. Our society asks, "How high are you? What is your position?" Christ asks, "How low are you? Are you washing one another's feet?" The following poem is a challenge to me; how does it affect you?

> You know, Lord, how I serve You
> with great emotional fervor in the limelight.
> You know how eagerly I speak for You at a Women's
> Club.
> You know my genuine enthusiasm at a Bible study.
> But how would I react, I wonder,
> if You pointed to a basin of water
> and asked me to wash the calloused feet
> of a bent and wrinkled old woman
> day after day, month after month,
> in a room where nobody saw and nobody knew? [8]

From Your Heart

How does the idea of "washing one another's feet" hit you? Do you have a serving spirit? What do you need to do to develop such a spirit?

Notes:
   1. Warren W. Wiersbe, *How to Be a Caring Christian* (Lincoln, NE: Good News Broadcasting Association, 1981), p. 17.
   2. Wiersbe, *How to Be a Caring Christian,* p. 16.
   3. Bryant, May 14.
   4. Chambers, p. 56.
   5. Richard Hooker, quoted by Gray and Adams, vol. 2, p. 467.
   6. Cowman, *Streams—2,* p. 253.
   7. Chambers, p. 54.
   8. Ruth Harms Calkin, quoted in "Selected Illustrations from *Bible Illustrator.*"

Forgive One Another

"And be ye kind one to another, tenderhearted, forgiving one another, even as God for Christ's sake hath forgiven you"
(Ephesians 4:32).

Forty-nine thousand new lawsuits are filed every day in the United States. Mates can't forgive one another; employees won't forgive; neighbors won't forgive. The end result—lawsuits! Less extreme cases of unforgiveness are revealed in crippling fears, outbursts of anger, tension in the home, apathy, silence and indifference, and distrust. Americans spend over one billion dollars on tranquilizers and antidepressant drugs, trying to cope with their internal anxieties. Doctors agree that deep-rooted resentments and bitterness affect our physical well-being and cause many chronic physical disorders.

Few people will admit they have an unforgiving spirit because that would imply they are personally responsible. They are more likely to talk about being hurt, shifting the blame to someone else, insinuating they are helpless victims. God reminds us over and over in His Word that we are to forgive others the same way He forgives us. When we won't or don't forgive, we are not Christlike. We will learn in this lesson why, when and how to forgive.

Before you start your study, I want you to examine yourself. Your honesty will determine how much you will profit from this lesson.

I often tell others how _____ has hurt me.

I cannot thank God for _____.

Whenever I think of _____, I still feel angry.

If _____ 's name comes up, I will probably have some sly remark to make.

I secretly am waiting for _____ to have to pay for the hurt he or she caused me.

If you wrote a name in any of these blanks, you have not forgiven the one who has hurt you.

Some of you may not have experienced a deep hurt. Maybe you have never been rejected by a mate or loved one, stabbed in the back by a person who was supposed to be your friend, or lied about. But someday you may! You are a blessed person if you can learn how to handle your hurts before they come.

> *". . . Forgiveness is something you train for in the easy times and in the small things so that you can perform graciously in the difficult times."* [1]

Why must we forgive?

1. It goes against our old nature to forgive those who have hurt us. Why must we forgive whether we feel like it or not?
   Matthew 6:14 and 15

   Ephesians 4:32

   2 Corinthians 2:5–11

2. (a) Think about the person who has hurt you; what is his or her sin?

   (b) Look at your unforgiving spirit; what is your sin?

(c) Which sin is worse?

"I realized that God looks at all sin the same and for me to judge one sin being greater than another, well, I was playing God. God is not partial, and He hated my sin just as much as He hated my husband's sin." [2]

We will never feel like forgiving; Satan will see to that. We must forgive whether we feel like it or not if we want to be Christlike.

3. We must forgive others the same way Christ forgives us. How is God's forgiveness described in Psalm 103:3 and 12 and Isaiah 43:25?

4. Based on how God forgives, how should we forgive?

"Remember: Forgiveness is not forgetting. It is a transaction in which I release my debtor from the obligation to repay his debt." [3]

---

5. Matthew 18:21–35 is a good picture of how we want forgiveness but often hesitate in giving forgiveness. Read these verses and then study the illustrations on page 86 to help you better understand the parable. Explain what happened between the master, the unmerciful servant, and the friend of the servant.

Servant One: $2,937,500   Servant Two: $16

"In Bible times, serious consequences awaited those who could not pay their debts. A person lending money could seize the borrower who couldn't pay and force him or his family to work until the debt was paid. The debtor could also be thrown into prison, or his family could be sold into slavery to help pay off the debt. It was hoped that the debtor, while in prison, would sell off his landholdings or that relatives would pay the debt. If not, the debtor could remain in prison for life."[4]

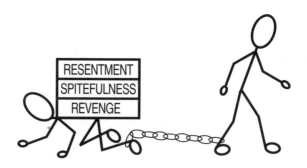

6. How does this illustration relate to us?

It is hard to forgive, but to live with the consequences of not forgiving is harder yet!

"Unforgiveness is to the spirit what disease is to the physical body. Unforgiveness debilitates, slowly and steadily. It gradually controls more and more. It begins to determine what we do and who we are. It virtually takes our future captive. . . .

Forgiveness liberates. It's like unhooking a ball and chain from our ankles —releasing us to truly enjoy the Christian life as God intended." [5]

---

7. What debts has your Master, the Lord Jesus Christ, forgiven you lately? Whom do you need to forgive? Write the person's initials on this blank line. _____

8. Do you have a right to withhold forgiveness? Will you ask God to give you a forgiving heart?

When must we forgive?

In a baseball game, three strikes and you're out. In the game of life, how many strikes does the offender get before we call him out? God's standards are much different from ours.

9. When and how often must we forgive someone when the person just keeps failing? Read Matthew 18:21 and 22.

10. Do the Matthew verses mean that at 491 you no longer have to forgive?

"Peter thought he was showing great faith and love when he offered to forgive at least seven times. After all, the rabbis taught that three times was sufficient.

> Our Lord's reply, 'Until seventy times seven'
> (490 times) must have startled Peter. Who could
> keep count for that many offenses? But that was
> exactly the point Jesus was making. Love 'keeps
> no record of wrongs' (1 Cor. 13:5, NIV). By the time
> we have forgiven a brother that many times, we
> are in the habit of forgiving." [6]

11. What lesson is taught in Matthew 5:22–24?

12. What if someone doesn't ask for forgiveness? Do you still
    have to forgive that person? Why?

How can we forgive?
We must take an honest look inside ourselves.

Before we can begin the process of forgiveness, we
must admit we have been hurt. Review in your mind what
and whom you need to forgive.

13. After you admit to yourself that you have been hurt,
    what else do you need to admit? Read Psalm 51:3.

We must, by an act of our wills, choose to forgive.

We must choose to forgive whether we feel like it or
not. Our decision to forgive must take precedence over our
faulty feelings. Forgiveness, like love, is not a feeling but a
choice.

14. What other characteristics must you choose to display
    in the forgiveness process? Read Ephesians 4:32.

We must choose not to seek revenge.

We must not listen to our old nature that desires revenge. We must refuse to punish or return hurt for hurt.

15. What example did Christ give us to follow when others intentionally hurt Him? Read Luke 23:34.

"Forgiving might be easier if we could merely forget the offense (and perhaps, the offender!). But forgetting, in the sense of having a blank mind regarding the offense, is not necessary in order to forgive. We forgive others as God forgives us when we commit ourselves never to bring up the offense again, to practice kindness to the offender, to attempt to understand his struggles, and to remember that we ourselves are forgiven people." [7]

We must show mercy.

16. James 2:13 says those who show no mercy will not receive mercy. What is one way mercy shows itself? Read 1 Peter 4:8.

We must help the one who hurt us rebuild his or her life.

Forgiveness is not a onetime decision; you may have to repeat the process several times before you can truly forgive. Once you know you are freed from your unforgiving spirit, you must do more than show mercy to the one who hurt you; you must help that person rebuild her life. However, this can be done only with one who is truly repentant and sorry for her offense. If it was a major offense, she will live with the consequences. You can help her lighten her load by saying what Joseph did, "Ye thought evil against me; but God meant it unto good . . ." (Genesis 50:20).

Joseph's life is a beautiful picture of a man forgiving, showing mercy, and helping to rebuild the lives of those who hurt him. You can read the story of Joseph's life in Genesis 37—50.

17. Joseph had every right, humanly speaking, to punish his brothers for selling him into slavery, but he didn't. Describe the final scene between Joseph and his brothers. Read Genesis 50:18–21.

"Until we forgive, we cannot begin to heal. Resentment is like holding a cactus. As long as we clutch it to ourselves, the spines will dig their way into our spirits and infect every part of our lives. There's no sense in even beginning to remove the spines until we put their source away, because as long as we keep on holding it, we cause additional damage." [8]

♡ *From My Heart*

I should be an authority on forgiveness; I sure have had a lot of practice the last few years. But I'm not! I still struggle with it just as much as you do. Yet I have learned to forgive by an act of my will. I choose to do it because I want to be Christlike, and I do it to free myself from bitterness and resentment. You may be asking the question so many ask, "If I forgive today, how can I be sure the bitterness and resentment won't come back tomorrow?" My simple answer is, "Practice the presence of God in your life each day." Here are my suggestions:

• Spend time in God's Word each day. Read Psalms when you are in turmoil. Choose one verse that is especially meaningful to you and write down what you learned from it.

• Talk to God each day. Thank Him for helping you yesterday, and remind Him you need His help and strength again today to keep a forgiving spirit.

• Meditate on God's Word each day. When negative, bitter thoughts enter your mind, replace them with positive promises from God's Word. I use the "Why Sink When You Can Swim" verses on pages 49 and 50 of my book *Trials— Don't Resent Them as Intruders.*

I must constantly remind myself, "When I won't forgive a person, I become a slave to that person." I want to be free! Don't you?

From Your Heart

Whom do you need to forgive? What are you going to do about it? When are you going to do it? Why not do it today?

Notes:
1. Gail MacDonald, p. 92.

2. "I Wouldn't Trade Any of the Pain," *Spirit of Revival* (August 1993), p. 11.

3. "Making It Personal," *Spirit of Revival* (August 1993), p. 33.

4. *Life Application Bible* (Wheaton, IL: Tyndale House Publishers, Inc., 1991), p. 1690.

5. Rex Rogers, "Forgiveness Unlimited," *The Messenger* (vol. 2, no. 1), p. 13.

6. Wiersbe, *The Bible Exposition Commentary,* vol. 1, p. 67.

7. Martin Clark, "Forgiving Is NOT Forgetting," *Cedarville Torch* (Fall 1989), p. 8.

8. Katherine Edwards, "Forgiveness and Healing" *The Messenger* (vol. 2, no. 1), p. 11.

Encourage One Another

*"Wherefore comfort [encourage] yourselves together, and
edify [build up] one another, even as also ye do"
(1 Thessalonians 5:11).*

Countless times I have been encouraged by another
woman's hug, an uplifting note, a gentle touch, a telephone
call, an invitation to lunch. Women talk together, pray together, and cry together. My husband, who often needs encouragement, seldom gets this kind of encouragement from
other men. I have tried to be an encouragement to people
for several years, but recently I have determined to do a better job. In the morning, after I've read my Bible and written
in my journal, I write the name of one person I want to encourage that day. That way I have it on my mind, and I can
think when and how I will encourage that person that day.

1. God says we are to "encourage one another." (The word
   translated "comfort" in 1 Thessalonians 5:11 in the King
   James Version may also be translated "encourage.")
   What do we often do that is just the opposite of this?
   Read Psalm 31:13.

> A careless word may kindle strife;
> A cruel word may wreck a life;
> A bitter word may hate instill;
> A brutal word may smite and kill.
> A gracious word may smooth the way;
> A joyous word may light the day;
> A timely word may lessen stress;
> A loving word may heal and bless.[1]

2. Which takes the most effort and intelligence: building up
   or tearing down? Why? Read Proverbs 11:11–13.

When you build something, you need tools. What tools can we use to encourage and build up one another? Five tools of great value in the building and encouraging process are words, listening, a touch, prayer, and our spiritual gifts.

Words
Spoken words

3. Read Ephesians 4:29–31. Paul was speaking to believers. He said, "Don't let corrupt words come from your mouth, but edifying words" (writer's paraphrase). In what manner were the corrupt words displayed?

4. Corrupt words tear down; edifying words build up. What three words in Ephesians 4:32 picture edifying, or building up?

> " 'Pit' and 'miry clay' [in Psalm 40:1–3] describe discouragement so well. We feel helpless, unable to rise, our feet trapped in a goo we cannot escape alone. Sometimes others may not realize how much a good word can be a rope to pull us up." [2]

5. What is a simple definition of grace?

6. Read Ephesians 4:29. How can our words "minister grace unto the hearers"?

7. A Japanese proverb says, "One kind word can warm up three winter months." Relate an incident in which

someone's encouraging words gave you the strength to keep going.

Don't say to the fellow who's down and out,
"Forget your troubles! Cheer up, old scout!"
But give him a wholesome, friendly hand,
And say, "I'm sorry—I understand."

The saddest thing in life, maybe,
Will happen—who knows? to you and me,
And it won't be in us to calmly smile
Or put it aside for a little while.

So cheer him over the roughest spot
With sympathy, for he needs a lot.
For many a heart that's tired and broken
Longs for a word that is never spoken.

It is fine to know, at the close of day,
That you helped someone in a human way.
So give him a wholesome, friendly hand,
And say, "I'm sorry—I understand." [3]

God's Word

8. The Word of God can be a continual source of encouragement to hurting people. With whom could you use the following verses?
   Psalm 55:22

   1 Corinthians 15:58

   Joshua 1:8

   Philippians 4:11

9. When people are facing problems and need building up, why is God's Word more effective than your words or ideas? Read Hebrews 4:12.

God's Word
To the weary pilgrim, I am a good staff.
To the one who sits in gloom, I am a glorious light.
To those who stoop beneath heavy burdens, I am
    sweet rest.
To him who has lost his way, I am a safe guide.
To those who have been hurt by sin, I am a healing
    balm.
To the discouraged, I whisper glad messages of hope.
To those who are distressed by the storms of life,
    I am an anchor.
To those who suffer in lonely solitude, I am a cool,
    soft hand resting on a fevered brow.
O, child of man, to best defend me, just use me! [4]

Written words

10. Why can written words of encouragement sometimes be more effective than spoken words?
2 Corinthians 10:1

Proverbs 25:25

"Make writing convenient for you. One person I know keeps a supply of post cards in her Bible. Sometimes during her devotional times she recalls someone she wants to encourage—and then writes something brief. Another puts notepaper in her car's glove compartment or purse. When she has a spare moment—while waiting in the car or

> *for a meeting to start—she jots a message to*
> *somebody whom God has put on her heart."* [5]

11. If you have a hard time writing what you want to say, what is another alternative available for encouraging others?

Listening

12. Someone has called listening "silent love." What kind of person is especially helped by a listening ear?

13. How does Proverbs 25:20 relate to listening to someone with a heavy heart?

> *"Most people don't want advice. They can identify*
> *their own problems; they may even know what to*
> *do about them. Yet all of us long for someone to*
> *whom we can pour out our hearts."* [6]

14. Someone said, "When grief is freshest, words should be the fewest." Why should we be careful in using Romans 8:28 when a tragedy first strikes?

It does a heap o' good sometimes,
    to go a little slow,
To say a word o' comfort
    to th' man that's stubbed his toe.[7]

A Touch

15. Jesus often extended His hand to people and touched them. What happened to many of them when He touched them? Read Mark 1:31; 5:25–29.

16. How can a touch or a hug be a healing and encouraging ministry?

". . . Every time you reach out to another human being who is in mourning, touch him gently. . . . Try to feel his pain and recognize his needs. That's what comfort is all about." [8]

Prayer

17. How were Paul's prayers of thanksgiving an encouragement to his friends? Read Ephesians 1:15, 16; Philippians 1:3; Colossians 1:3; 2 Timothy 1:3.

18. How do you feel when a person tells you she is praying for a particular need in your life?

"I am encouraged when I learn that I matter enough to others to occupy their conversations with God. It tells me our friendship is deep enough

to allow us to be open with one another. It shows
me they want to draw alongside my need. . . ." [9]

Spiritual Gifts

Romans 12:6–8 is one list of the spiritual gifts God gives to His children. We each have at least one gift. Look over the list and try to discern your spiritual gift or gifts.

Prophecy (preaching)—This is usually considered the gift given to pastors.

Ministry (serving)—Helping whenever and wherever needed.

Teaching—Making the Word of God understandable to others.

Exhortation (encouraging)—Those who use the tools mentioned in this lesson to build up others.

Giving—Being liberal with one's finances. If there is a special need, you can count on these people.

Rulers (leaders, administrators)—These people make good committee leaders.

Mercy (caring)—These people are good comforters.

19. If your gift is not exhortation or mercy, does that exclude you from encouraging others? Why? Read John 13:35.

From My Heart

It almost seems ironic that I should be writing a chapter on encouragement at this particular time in my life. It has been a long time since I have felt so discouraged. I keep thinking, "Are these books worth all the time and effort I put into them? Do I really want to keep writing?" Only the Lord knows what a hard time I'm having right now, and He not only knows—He cares! On one of those "down days" last week, the Lord laid it on the heart of a lady in Nebraska to write me an encouraging note. She had never met me and had no idea what was going on in my life. This is an excerpt from the note she wrote me:

> Dear Juanita,
> . . . I personally attend one study and lead another using your guides. They are powerful tools—I love to share them with ladies I know all over our state. God is doing a mighty work in our little group.
> In quiet moments I think of you.
> In excited moments I thank God for you.
> I just wanted to let you know what a blessing you have been.
> I love you in Christ.

Thank you, friend. I just want to let you know what a blessing and encouragement your note was to me.

Mark Twain said he could live three weeks on one compliment. We must remember "Death and life are in the power of the tongue" (Proverbs 18:21). Who could you revive with a few encouraging words?

From Your Heart

Are you a good encourager? Which of the five tools are easiest for you to use? What could you do to encourage someone today?

I trust we have learned the value of caring for one another in these lessons. It is time we start putting into practice some of the things we have learned about relationships by encouraging and helping one another. I'm going to try harder—will you?

Thanks for letting me share my heart with you.

Juanita

Notes:
1. Gariepy, p. 92.
2. Jeanne Doering, *The Power of Encouragement* (Chicago: Moody Press, 1982), p. 40.
3. Nan Terrell Reed, *Nuggets* (February 1965).
4. Source unknown.
5. Doering, p. 52.
6. Christine Suguitan, "The Gift of Listening," *Moody* (December 1993), p. 23.
7. James William Foley, quoted by Marilyn Cram Donahue, *The Pearl Is in the Oyster* (Wheaton, IL: Tyndale House Publishers, Inc., 1980), p. 29.
8. Donahue, p. 35.
9. Doering, p. 120.

LEADER'S GUIDE

SUGGESTIONS FOR LEADERS

The effectiveness of a group Bible study usually depends on two things: (1) the leader herself; and (2) the ladies' commitment to prepare beforehand and interact during the study. You cannot totally control the second factor, but you have total control over the first one. These brief suggestions will help you be an effective Bible study leader.

You will want to prepare each lesson a week in advance. During the week, read supplemental material and look for illustrations in the everyday events of your life as well as in the lives of others.

Encourage the ladies in the Bible study to complete each lesson before the meeting itself. This preparation will make the discussion more interesting. You can suggest that ladies answer two or three questions a day as part of their daily Bible reading time rather than trying to do the entire lesson at one sitting.

You may also want to encourage the ladies to memorize the key verse for each lesson. (This is the verse that is printed in italics at the start of each lesson.) If possible, print the verses on 3" x 5" cards to distribute each week. If you cannot do this, suggest that the ladies make their own cards and keep them in a prominent place throughout the week.

The physical setting in which you meet will have some bearing on the study itself. An informal circle of chairs, chairs around a table, someone's living room or family room—these types of settings encourage people to relax and participate. In addition to an informal setting, create an atmosphere in which ladies feel free to participate and be themselves.

During the discussion time, here are a few things to observe.

• Don't do all the talking. This is not designed to be a lecture.

• Encourage discussion on each question by adding ideas and questions.

• Don't discuss controversial issues that will divide the group. (Differences of opinion are healthy; divisions are not.)

• Don't allow one lady to dominate the discussion. Use statements such as these to draw others into the study: "Let's hear from someone on this side of the room" (the side opposite the dominant talker); "Let's hear from someone who has not shared yet today."

• Stay on the subject. The tendency toward tangents is always possible in a discussion. One of your responsibilities as the leader is to keep the group on the track.

• Don't get bogged down on a question that interests only one person.

You may want to use the last fifteen minutes of the scheduled time for prayer. If you have a large group of ladies, divide into smaller groups for prayer. You could call this the "Share and Care Time."

If you have a morning Bible study, encourage the ladies to go out for lunch with someone else from time to time. This is a good way to get acquainted with new ladies. Occasionally you could plan a time when ladies bring their own lunches or salads to share and eat together. These things help promote fellowship and friendship in the group.

The formats that follow are suggestions only. You can plan your own format, use one of these or adapt one of these to your needs.

2-hour Bible Study

10:00—10:15 Coffee and fellowship time

10:15—10:30 Get-acquainted time

Have two ladies take five minutes each to tell something about themselves and their families.

Also use this time to make announcements and, if appropriate, take an offering for the baby-sitters.

10:30—11:45 Bible study

Leader guides discussion of the questions in the day's lesson.

11:45—12:00 Prayer time

2-hour Bible Study

10:00—10:45 Bible lesson

Leader teaches a lesson on the content of the material. No discussion during this time.

10:45—11:00 Coffee and fellowship

11:00—11:45 Discussion time

Divide into small groups with an appointed leader for each group. Discuss the questions in the day's lesson.

11:45—12:00 Prayer time

1¹/₂-hour Bible Study

10:00—10:30 Bible study

Leader guides discussion of half the questions in the day's lesson.

10:30—10:45 Coffee and fellowship

10:45—11:15 Bible study

Leader continues discussion of the questions in the day's lesson.

11:15—11:30 Prayer time

ANSWERS FOR LEADER'S USE

Information inside parentheses ( ) is additional instruction for the group leader.

LESSON 1

1. No, she can't. God said if we really love Him, we will love others also. Just as oil and water don't mix, neither do love and hate. Oil always rises above the water, and hate always rises above love.

2. Christ was at the Last Supper with His disciples, just before He went to Calvary.

3. Leviticus 19:18.

4. We are born with a sinful, selfish nature, and we love ourselves by nature. We are to love others the same way we love ourselves and look out for our own interests.

5. To love others the way Christ loves us. This is a giving, selfless love.

6. No. This command is for all believers who desire to truly follow the Lord.

7. People will know we are followers of Christ because of our Christlike love.

8. He died for us—the ultimate sacrifice.

9. Possible answers are patient; tenderhearted; generous; humble; modest; courteous; unselfish; mild-tempered; positive; sincere; honest; tolerant; trusting; expectant; persevering; faithful.

10. (Ask the ladies to be honest in their evaluation of themselves.)

11. We must be born again and have the Holy Spirit dwelling in us and controlling us.

12. (Ask the ladies to share some of their experiences.)

13. Strength is available through Jesus Christ. We can do the things Christ commands us to do when we exchange our strength for His supernatural strength. The word "renew" in Isaiah 40:31 means "exchange."

14. We willingly and deliberately choose to treat others the way Christ treats us. His love is always unconditional and sacrificial. Love is not a feeling but a choice. We *choose* to love like Christ loves.

LESSON 2

1. (a) The verses before and after it in the Scriptural text. (b) To disregard the verses before and after a verse. You can make a verse say anything you want it to say if you take it away from the verses that precede and follow it. If we read Matthew 7:1 alone, it would indicate we should never judge. We need to consider the verse in its context.

2. (a) Jesus was preaching to the people, including the disciples. (b) The Sermon on the Mount.

3. To pass judgment and give the verdict on another person or her behavior.

4. (Personal answers. Most women will think the problem is widespread because we all know we are guilty of judging.)

5. The same way we judge others. If we are harsh in our judgment of others, we will receive the same treatment; e.g., a person may say, "Don't listen to her; she never has a good word to say about anyone." The person is being judged in the same way she judged.

6. They weren't perfect, but they expected others to be perfect. They were looking at a speck in their brother's eye, but they had logs in their own eyes.

7. These verses condemn self-righteous judgment. We need to judge ourselves before we judge others.

8. Judge others the way we would like to be judged—with understanding and fairness.

9. False teachers need to be exposed for what they are.

10. Exercise church discipline in the case of an immoral member.

11. Some Christians were judging others as less spiritual or not as good as themselves if they didn't do things just like they did. Some

Roman Christians felt right in eating meat that had been offered to idols; others thought such a practice was wrong. The Christians who didn't eat the meat felt they were more spiritual.

12. (Have the ladies share their thoughts. Answers will probably include things such as the Bible translation another person does or doesn't use, the use of taped music in church, places people do or don't go, what people do on Sundays.)

13. It can destroy the work of God.

14. Judging based on principle means a determination is made based on clear Biblical teaching. We often judge others based on our own personal preference, which is not the same as a Biblical conviction.

15. (Let the ladies share their answers. Here is one example: The Bible condemns sexual sin [Eph. 5:3]; whether to sing praise choruses or worship hymns is personal preference.)

16. A self-righteous, hypocritical, judgmental attitude that tears down others to build up oneself.

17. (a) Before partaking of the Lord's supper, or communion. (b) No; we need to judge ourselves daily.

18. Confess it and forsake it.

LESSON 3

1. Definition: sympathetic, friendly, gentle, benevolent, and generous. A kind person shows love in little things and is gentle and sympathetic in reaching out to others.

2. (Ask the ladies to share their answers.)

3. Being tenderhearted and forgiving.

4. It is the opposite of hard-hearted. Unkind people are usually hard-hearted, uncaring, and selfish. Tenderhearted people are kind, caring, and generous.

5. We don't deserve Christ's kindness and forgiveness, but He keeps showing us mercy each time we fail. If we want to be Christlike, we must treat others the way Christ treats us.

6. (Ask the ladies to share their answers. The idea is that showing kindness is more effective in winning people than rebuking them. Or, it takes a heart for others to win others' hearts.)

7. We must put on kindness like we would put on a dress. We must choose, by an act of our will, to show kindness. In situations where we could easily be unkind, we must plan ahead of time to be kind. We must constantly be thinking how our words will be received before we start talking.

8. We cannot demonstrate godly love to others if we do not have a kind, tenderhearted, forgiving spirit.

9. We will treat others the way we would like to be treated. We will be sensitive to the suffering and sorrow of others and look for ways of relieving that suffering.

10. Both groups are kind to those who are kind to them and courteous to those who reciprocate.

11. Kindness generally grows best when treated rudely. We wouldn't have to work on kindness if everyone were always kind to us.

12. The fruit of the Spirit rather than the works of the flesh.

13. This verse refers to a wife's conduct before an unsaved husband. The idea is, "Reach him with your kind life without saying a word." The principle applies in other areas of life as well. Kind actions are often more beneficial than lots of words.

14. It is better to be kind than to talk about kindness.

15. They were killed in a battle against the Philistines.

16. Jonathan had been David's best friend. David wanted to be kind to someone in Saul's family for Jonathan's sake.

17. Mephibosheth was Jonathan's son. He was crippled because a nurse had dropped him when they were fleeing after the death of Saul and Jonathan. Mephibosheth was five years old at the time.

18. Mephibosheth received all of Saul's land along with servants to care for it. Mephibosheth became as one of David's sons and ate at David's table.

19. It is an example of how David, a man after God's own heart (Acts 13:22), acted in contrast to the prevailing custom of the day, which was to kill any living family members of a slain, rival king. Also, all Old Testament accounts were written that we might learn from them (Rom. 15:4).

20. As kindness done to Him.

LESSON 4

1. To surrender my will to the will of another.

2. Verse 19—joy; verse 20—thankfulness; verse 21—submission.

3. Jesus Christ.

4. (a) The carnal mind and the spiritual mind. (b) The spiritual mind.

5. Above all others; supreme in power and rank; independent of all others.

6. Psalm 115:3—He does as He pleases. Isaiah 14:27—Once God sets His plan in action, no man can stop it. Proverbs 16:9—We make our plans, but God can change them. Lamentations 3:37—Nothing happens unless God allows it.

7. (Have the ladies share their answers. The idea is that recognizing God's sovereignty makes it easier for us to submit to Him.)

8. God commands it. It leads to the enjoyment of a long life. It is a way of finding favor with God and man.

9. Wife—submit to her husband, willingly following his leadership in Christ. Husband—love his wife as his own body, putting away his interests to care for hers.

10. Checks by the second and fourth reasons.

11. If he is unsaved, her submission may help bring him to Christ. In any woman, submission develops a meek and quiet spirit, and that helps to make harmony in the home.

12. Employees, obey your employer; give him your best each day. Don't work hard just when the boss is watching; always work hard because this is the will of God and you want to please Christ. Christ is watching you; you will be repaid for each good thing you do.

13. Pray about it, and humbly submit. God will give you grace if you give your burden to Him.

14. God determines who government leaders will be.

15. Government is ordained of God. If we do not submit to governmental authority, we are disobeying God.

16. Pay taxes; obey speed limits; obey local ordinances (e.g., get a building permit for a home-improvement project); see that children obey curfews. (Other answers are also possible.)

17. He is the shepherd, and they are the flock. He is responsible for their care and feeding, but he is not to "lord it" over them.

18. Love, respect, and submission.

19. Rebellion or resistance.

20. (No answers are necessary.)

LESSON 5

1. A sister (or brother) in Christ who has sinned.

2. "Overtaken" pictures a person's being off guard in contrast to the premeditated practice of evil.

3. Restore the person in the spirit of meekness.

4. Galatians 6:1 follows the description of the Spirit-controlled person in Galatians 5:22–26. The person who seeks to restore a sinning brother needs to be a Spirit-controlled person.

5. Meekness.

6. It is not weakness but power under control. It is a humble, submissive spirit.

7. It is a medical term, referring to such things as setting a bone. To restore a person is to help her get back to where she was before she fell.

8. It takes wisdom from God and knowledge of His Word to know how to help a sinning sister. If a person rushes in and uses human wisdom and reasoning, she may do more harm than good.

9. A spirit of pride.

10. She realizes she could just as easily have been the sinner rather than the restorer; "there but for the grace of God go I."

11. Watch yourself; you might find yourself in similar circumstances someday.

12. Hide God's Word in our heart.

13. We are commanded to bear one another's burdens.

14. To fulfill the law of Christ.

15. The command to love one another.

16. It deceives us and makes us feel we are more spiritual than we really are. I say to myself, "I'm beyond that; I could never be enticed into that kind of sin; I would never allow myself to get so low."

17. If someone is worse than me, it makes me look better.

18. Ourselves. We should rejoice in our works without comparing them to another's works.

19. Family problems, health problems, financial pressures, work or loss-of-work pressures.

20. Answers may include spend time with a hurting person; send a note or card; provide a meal; baby-sit so parents can go out; help financially if possible; provide love and understanding.

LESSON 6

1. We can pretend we love others, but God wants our love to go beyond pretense and politeness. Sincere love forgets about self and centers on others.

2. Doing something in a spirit of hypocrisy or with empty flattery.

3. Employer—We butter up the boss, hoping for a promotion or raise. Employer to employee—The boss thinks if he tells the worker how great the worker is, the worker will work harder and make more money for the boss. Wealthy relative—Maybe old Aunt Sally will leave me some of her money if I tell her how wonderful she is.

4. It can ruin us and others.

5. Pride takes over. When pride consumes a life, destruction will eventually come.

6. They say, "I can't do anything; you're so good and I'm so bad."

7. He said, "I am not eloquent; I'm not a good speaker."

8. "I made your tongue and mouth; now use it and obey Me!"

9. Preferring one before another is partiality; preferring one another is thinking of others ahead of yourself.

10. More important.

11. Love and humility.

12. (Have the ladies share their illustrations. Here is one scenario: You have done most of the work on a committee. It appears to others that the lady heading up the committee did most of the work. You keep your mouth shut and let her get the honor and praise.)

13. Abraham let Lot have first choice of the land, and Lot chose the best land.

14. We must have the attitude, "I want God to get the glory and honor, not me. I want Christ to be preeminent in my life."

15. For the work they do. Spiritual leaders are accountable to God for their ministries.

16. In Heaven, at the Judgment Seat of Christ.

17. On quality, "of what sort it is" (1 Cor. 3:13). God assesses our motives and faithfulness (1 Cor. 4:2).

18. God will one day reward that person.

LESSON 7

1. You must know the God of all comfort and have experienced His comfort in your life.

2. There is no limit in God's ability to comfort. In what area do you need comfort? The word "all" covers that need. We can go only so far in comforting others, but God's comfort is limitless.

3. What you know about the God of all comfort is where your message starts. If you don't really know God in a personal, intimate way, you won't have much to share.

4. Isaiah 66:13—God can give us the comfort our mothers gave us when we cuddled up in their laps after getting hurt. 2 Corinthians 7:6—God knows when we are down and discouraged, when no one else knows or even cares. He can lift us up again. John 14:16—If we know Christ as Savior, our Comforter is always close at hand. He is in us and always with

us. Isaiah 49:16—God has us in the palm of His hand. It is impossible for Him to forget us. Romans 15:4—We can have hope and comfort, but we won't have it unless we believe what God has said in His Word.

5. We must have a joyful contentment when things are good and when things are bad. It is not what we say that gives a message, but what we are.

6. God promises comfort through the Scriptures. No other book can deliver on that promise.

7. We all have troubles; some have more, some have less, but we all have them. If we have experienced God's comfort in our troubles, we have something to share with others.

8. Sympathy is compassion for another person's troubles or suffering. Empathy is not just an emotional feeling of compassion for another person's suffering, it is also an intellectual compassion. We know how another person feels because we have experienced a form of the same suffering.

9. No, we don't have to have had the same experience to comfort, but we do have to be able to share how God has comforted us.

10. She can empathize with the hurting person, saying, "I know how you feel; I've been there, but I made it through. God can help you just like He helped me."

11. We must remember that anguish and pain in the heart produce the words. Sometimes the words are a way of releasing the tension and frustration of a painful situation.

12. Psalm 23:4—facing death. Psalm 27:1—fear. Hebrews 13:5—loneliness. Psalm 27:10—broken relationships. Philippians 4:19—financial loss. Psalm 69:20 and 33—broken heart.

13. (Ask the ladies to share other verses they use.)

14. Psalm 3:3—shield; Psalm 40:17—help and deliverer; Matthew 6:9—Father; Isaiah 9:6—counselor; Psalm 91:2—refuge and fortress; Psalm 71:3—rock and fortress.

15. Study God's Word so you will know verses of comfort to share with people.

16. Just sit with the person, hold her hand, pray with her, and leave. If it is a close friend, just be there and talk only if she wants to talk. If there are no answers to give, don't try—just be silent. Job's friends were comforters until they started talking and trying to give him reasons for his troubles. Sometimes God doesn't tell us why!

LESSON 8

1. The practice of entertaining with kindness and courtesy; generous and cordial reception of guests.

2. Through other people's opening their homes to them.

3. Whatever was done for Christ's brethren was the same as doing it for Christ.

4. Poor and needy, strangers, and fellow believers.

5. The needy person might be someone who just moved to town and needs a temporary place to stay. Or she might be a college student who

needs a place to live in the summer. A stranger might be a missionary or a visiting evangelist or guest speaker.

6. She urged Paul and his companions to stay in her home during their ministry in Philippi. They returned to her home after having been in jail. Lydia was able to help strangers feel at home!

7. We need to have other believers in our homes so our friendships can go beyond a Sunday morning "hello" and we can learn to love one another.

8. Other Christians who are not in our circles; e.g., too liberal or too legalistic; our unsaved neighbors and friends; those out of our class; e.g., too rich or too poor.

9. We may be missing an opportunity to develop a new friendship that we would never experience otherwise. Often these visits develop into lifelong relationships.

10. These reasons are common: my house is not nice enough or big enough; I'm not a good cook, or I don't like to cook; I don't want others messing up my house; my house is a mess; we don't have enough money to entertain.

11. We could entertain to impress others with what we have. True hospitality is sharing with others what we have, whether it is little or much.

12. A kind and courteous attitude; not a grudging spirit that displays to the guests, "I wish I didn't have to do this!"

13. We need to step into our guests' shoes and treat our guests the way we would like to be treated if we were in their home.

14. He considers it a labor of love, done in His name. He will not forget it.

15. You've been missing a blessing. We always get back more than we give when we have people in our home. (At least most of the time! We've probably all had a few experiences we would just as soon forget.)

16. (Have the ladies share their ideas.)

17. If you don't plan ahead, you'll be too tired or harried to enjoy your guests. Don't wait until the last minute to clean the house and shop.

LESSON 9

1. Any form of untruth conveyed in word or deed.

2. Every person is born with a sin nature; he sins because he is a sinner. Lying is sin.

3. Lying started with the father of lies, Satan.

4. It is impossible for God to lie.

5. Satan told Eve she wouldn't really die if she disobeyed God and ate the fruit.

6. We twist the truth a little and say, "God doesn't really mean that, does He? After all, this is the twenty-first century!"

7. Fear of being caught when they have done something wrong.

8. (a) They brought to the apostles the money from the sale of some property. The money was to be used to meet needs in the church. They represented their gift as the total amount received, when, in fact, it was only part of the amount. (b) It made them look better in other people's

eyes; e.g., "Did you hear how much Ananias and Sapphira contributed?"

9. He said Sarah was his sister, which was half-true since she was his half-sister. The problem was what he omitted: Sarah was also his wife.

10. Because half-truths have some truth in them, it is more difficult to discern the falsehood.

11. A false witness is one of the seven things that are an abomination to God.

12. The trial of Jesus Christ.

13. When we tell a story we do not know is true, we run the risk of slandering a person's character. Even if the story is true, by the time it has passed over the tongues of two or three people, the story may not be the same as it started.

14. We should not retaliate.

15. Issac was old and feeble and almost blind. Rebekah and Jacob took advantage of him by tricking him into believing that Jacob was Esau. They disguised Jacob with a goatskin covering so he could steal his brother Esau's birthright.

16. They may misuse the finances and not actually tell where they are spending money. They may pretend to be too busy to take care of the house or cook when they are out running around and doing other things. They pretend they don't feel well to avoid having sex.

17. Pride! Pride loves to talk about itself and tell others what great things it has done.

18. Their words and actions didn't match.

19. At church. People sing, "I'll Go Where You Want Me to Go, Dear Lord," but don't mean it. Families walk into church smiling and acting as if they are so happy, but their homelife is "hell on earth."

20. I will never deny you! Peter was heartbroken when he realized he had not kept his word (Matt. 26:75).

21. The promise to live together until death.

22. Proverbs 20:17—guilt. Proverbs 19:5—punishment. Hebrews 12:6—chastening.

23. Put it out of your life by learning to walk a Spirit-controlled life instead of a self-controlled life. A self-controlled life is filled with pride, deceit and lying.

LESSON 10

1. The roads were dusty, and the people commonly wore sandals. It was a courtesy to wash guests' dirty feet.

2. A household servant.

3. Christ is the King of Kings, the Lord of Lords. He had everything in His hands to do as He pleased, yet He placed in His hands a servant's towel.

4. On His knees—a very humbling position.

5. Jesus' betrayal by Judas and Jesus' crucifixion.

6. (Have the ladies share their experiences.)

7. When a person is born again, she is permanently cleansed from the penalty of sin (Rev. 1:5; Titus 3:5), but she needs daily cleansing (i.e., feet only) for the daily defilement of sin (1 John 1:7–9).

8. You know I am your Lord and Master, yet I was willing to wash your feet. I want you to do the same for one another.

9. No. Jesus was teaching the disciples to be willing to serve one another.

10. Both passages describe servanthood. Christ willingly humbled Himself and became a servant. He put Himself at the feet of others to serve them.

11. A prideful, competitive spirit. They wanted to know which of them was the greatest.

12. His humility was a rebuke to their selfishness and pride. He wanted to teach them that the ones who are the greatest are the ones who will serve others.

13. It means we must humble ourselves before others and take on the role of a servant: helping others, ministering to others, being a blessing and refreshment to others. It means being Christlike!

14. The pastor wanted to remind the young man that he was going to be a servant not to be served.

15. (Some ladies may be willing to share their answers.)

16. Serving for personal glory and praise, not for God's glory. The root of this kind of service is pride: "Look how much I do!"

17. Learn to have the mind of Christ; learn to think like Christ would think—of others, not self. We must think of serving others instead of being served.

18. (Ask the ladies to answer honestly.)

19. Spend time just being available and listening; be available to do jobs we don't like to do; humble ourselves to forgive when we don't want to.

20. (Some of the ladies may want to share their experiences.)

21. As we get to know Christ more and more, we desire more and more to be like Him and to do His will. Humility and serving others are natural outgrowths of being Christlike.

LESSON 11

1. Matthew 6:14, 15—None of us is perfect enough that we will never fail and need forgiveness. So if we want to be forgiven, we must practice forgiveness. We get what we give: give forgiveness, get forgiveness. Luke 6:38 reminds us of this fact: "Give, and it shall be given unto you. . . . For with the same measure that ye mete withal it shall be measured to you again." Whatever "it" is that we give, "it" is what we get. Ephesians 4:32—If you don't feel like forgiving, do it because Christ commands you to do it. He says we are to forgive others the same way He forgives us. 2 Corinthians 2:5–11—We must forgive to prove our obedience and not give Satan an advantage in our lives. Most of the ground Satan gains in Christians' lives is due to their having an unforgiving spirit.

2. (a) and (b) (No answers are necessary.) (c) God does not list sins as big sins and little sins. Sin is sin in God's sight, and He hates it all. We must see our unforgiving spirit as the sin it is.

3. It is described as complete. God forgives completely; He removes the sin and remembers it no more.

4. We should forgive completely. True forgiveness wipes the slate

clean. It is a promise never to remind the person of his or her sin again.

5. The servant owed a debt so large he could never repay it. He humbled himself and fell on his knees and pled for mercy. The king had compassion on the servant and released him. But even more astounding, he forgave the three-million-dollar debt. After servant one was released, he met a friend (servant two) who owed him sixteen dollars. He demanded repayment! The king was furious when he found out. He reminded the servant of all he had forgiven and wanted to know why he wouldn't show the same mercy. The king delivered the servant to his tormentors until he repaid. (According to one source, a talent was worth $29,375 in today's currency, and a denarii was worth $.16, or the amount a laborer earned in a day.)

6. If we won't forgive someone, it is as if we are chained to the person and drag him with us wherever we go. We are constantly thinking about him, so he becomes our tormentor, and we are tormented with bitterness, spitefulness and revenge.

7. (Personal answers.)

8. (Ask the ladies to search their hearts.)

9. As often as is needed, even 70 x 7 or 490 times, if necessary.

10. No. You just keep forgiving and forgiving. You forgive so many times you lose track of the number.

11. You cannot have a right relationship with God when you have an unforgiving spirit.

12. Yes. The Bible doesn't say forgive when a person asks forgiveness; it just says forgive and get rid of your bitterness (Eph. 4:31, 32).

13. You must admit your unforgiving spirit is sin and realize God sees it.

14. Kindness and tenderheartedness.

15. He prayed, "Father, forgive them for they know not what they do." We must do the same. Praying for those who hurt us will help heal the hurt.

16. It covers the person's sin and doesn't tell everyone how the person treated you. Remember, we get what we give. Show mercy, get mercy. Servant one didn't show mercy to servant two, and he didn't get mercy in the final analysis.

17. Joseph's brothers were fearful Joseph would kill them. He said, "You meant to hurt me, but God used all the hurtful experiences for good. Don't be fearful; I will take care of you and your families."

LESSON 12

1. We say and do things to discourage one another. We destroy and tear down one another rather than build up each other.

2. It takes more effort to build up because it takes time to care and encourage in word and deed. To tear down a person takes no heart or mind, just an uncaring and destructive spirit.

3. In bitterness, wrath, anger, clamor, and speaking with malice.

4. Kind, tenderhearted, and forgiving.

5. Undeserved favor.

6. The idea in the verse is words that benefit the hearer. We can

benefit others by speaking kind words, encouraging words, sympathetic words.

7. (Ask two or three volunteers to share.)

8. Psalm 55:22—Someone who is carrying a heavy burden. 1 Corinthians 15:58—Someone who is discouraged and sees no fruit in her ministry. Joshua 1:8—Someone who needs to be encouraged to stay in the Word daily. Philippians 4:11—Someone dealing with discontentment.

9. God's Word is more powerful than our words. It can change a life as dramatically as a surgeon's knife can. It penetrates to the core of our moral and spiritual life.

10. 2 Corinthians 10:1—We may be less shy on paper than face-to-face with a person. Proverbs 25:25—A note or letter can refresh over and over. It can be read several times.

11. There are greeting cards for everything: Sorry You're Hurting, I Miss You, Why I Haven't Written, Just-to-let-you-know-I-care, and on and on. If you can't say it, use someone else's words. After the death of my father, I tried to send my mother a funny card every few weeks to cheer her up. One card I sent pictured people riding a roller coaster, and it said, "Life is sometimes like a roller coaster—it makes you want to puke!" It was funny but true.

12. Someone who is suffering much heartache and pain because of some great loss or tragedy in her life.

13. We need to try to understand how the person feels and feel with her. She doesn't need a cheerleader saying, "Cheer up; it could be worse." She needs a quiet, listening, and understanding person.

14. Many Christians know "all things work together for good," but they are not ready to hear it. Their hearts and minds are in too much turmoil to comprehend what God may be trying to accomplish in their lives.

15. They were healed.

16. A touch or a hug is a nonverbal way of saying "I care!"

17. The prayers were a means of expressing Paul's love for people.

18. It reminds me that others are helping to share my burden. Knowing someone cares enough to pray for me strengthens my faith.

19. I know from my own experience that not everyone is a good encourager. But we can all love one another. Knowing someone loves you is always a source of encouragement.